SHORT CUTS

INTRODUCTIONS TO FILM STUDIES

SHAKESPEARE ON FILM

SUCH THINGS AS DREAMS ARE MADE OF

CAROLYN JESS-COOKE

WALLFLOWER

LONDON and NEW YORK

A Wallflower Paperback

First published in Great Britain in 2007 by
Wallflower Press
6 Market Place, London W1W 8AF
www.wallflowerpress.co.uk

ISBN 978 1 905674 14 5

Book design by Rob Bowden Design

Printed in Great Britain by Antony Rowe Ltd, Chippenham, Wiltshire

CONTENTS

ACKNOWLEDGEMENTS

I would like to thank my colleagues at the University of Sunderland for their unceasing support during my research leave for this book. I am also grateful to Niall Richardson, Martin Shingler, Deborah Thomas and an anonymous reader for their trenchant comments on early chapter drafts. Thanks also to my students for their rewarding insights into embryonic versions of the critical concepts developed here. At Wallflower Press thanks to Jacqueline Downs for her rigorous editing and to Yoram Allon for his enthusiasm for the project. Gratitude to Mark Thornton Burnett, Clare McManus, Robert Shaughnessy and Ramona Wray for their guidance, mentoring and rigorously challenging feedback during my doctorate, which fuelled the fire for this book. Love and greatest indebtedness to my husband Jared and daughter Melody for their encouragement, inspiration, patience and support. This book is dedicated to them.

INTRODUCTION: HISTORICAL BEGINNINGS AND
CRITICAL CONTEXTS

This book provides an introductory companion to the study of Shakespeare on film. Since the first Shakespeare film appeared on screen in 1899, a vast number of academic enquiries, performance strategies, critical approaches and cultural dialogues have circulated around 'Bardic' cinema. Although early Shakespeare incarnations struggled with the move from stage to screen, the gradual development of narrative form and the relationship between film and literature has paved the way for a devotedly Shakespearean niche in the growing cinematic market. And, after almost three centuries as a cultural institution, Shakespeare provided cinema – seen at its beginning by its own inventors as a gimmick without value or future – with the cultural weight necessary for a sustainable global enterprise.

Who, or what, was Shakespeare?

There are few known historical facts about William Shakespeare (1564–1616), the individual generally assumed to be the author of 37 plays written and performed in England during the early modern period. From the time that Shakespeare's plays and poems entered scholarly terrain, a host of claims for alternative identities of the author have emerged, ranging from Christopher Marlowe (a contemporary playwright), Sir Francis Bacon (Lord Verulam), William Stanley (Sixth Earl of Derby), Edward de Vere (17th Earl of Oxford), to Queen Elizabeth I. While his identity as the plays' author remains in question, Shakespeare's *authority* as a cultural agent can be regarded in terms of a long-established network of historical conversations and textual revisions.

Historians generally agree on a number of facts: that Shakespeare was born in Stratford-upon-Avon in April 1564, was married at 18 to a pregnant Anne Hathaway, moved to London in the 1580s, and famously left only his second-best bed to his estranged wife in his will. In 1596, Shakespeare's only son, Hamnet, died at 11 years old, possibly as a result of the Bubonic Plague that was scything its way through the population of Europe. About two years later, Shakespeare composed a play about a man urged by the ghost of his murdered father to seek revenge by killing his father's murderer, who was also his stepfather. This play is *Hamlet*, one of the Bard's most famous plays which has been rendered for the screen approximately one hundred times. The apparent relations between *Hamlet*'s investments in father/son relationships and thematic interests in death and mourning – not to mention the similarity between the play's title and the name of Shakespeare's own son – are a primary example of the biographical connections threaded by scholars from the plays to construct Shakespearean 'facts'. Yet these connections are tenuous at best. The plot of *Hamlet* is based on a twelfth-century Danish legend, 'Amleth'. Another *Hamlet* source, the so-called *Ur-Hamlet*, has been said to overshadow the play in much the same way as the ghost of Old Hamlet. To the contrary of some Shakespearean scholarship, Shakespeare appeared to be less interested in directly expressing his own feelings or experiences than he was in re-appropriating established works.

The haunting of Hamlet by Old Hamlet serves as a general commentary on Shakespeare's plays and their subsequent filmic incarnations: with only two exceptions (*Love's Labours Lost* and *A Midsummer Night's Dream*), all of Shakespeare's plays are 'haunted' by previous sources. Shakespeare borrows, cribs, imitates, plagiarises, reworks, updates and blatantly pilfers from a number of noted classical authors and historians, such as Ovid, Holinshed, Horace, Seneca, Virgil, Plutarch, Homer, Plautus and Saxo the Grammarian. It is possibly this penchant for imitation that led to fellow playwright Robert Greene's public denouncement of Shakespeare in 1592 as 'an upstart crow'; a reference, of course, to a creature that steals the goods of others. Greene goes on to accuse Shakespeare as follows:

> [He is] beautified with our feathers, that with his *Tygers hart wrapt in a Players hyde*, supposes he is as well able to bombast out a blanke verse as the best of you: and beeing an absolute *Johannes*

factotum, is in his owne conceit the onely Shake-scene in a coun-
trey. (Greene 1592: n.p.)

Possibly damning at the time, Greene's published defamation inadvertently aided historians by advertising Shakespeare's status in the
London theatre at the end of the sixteenth century. As the pun 'Shake-
scene' suggests, this status was of particular import, and was apparently
threatening to other playwrights. Moreover, the publication underlines a
significant artistic dimension of the Bard that additionally accesses the
logic of Shakespearean cinema. By suggesting Shakespeare as possess-
ing a 'tiger's heart wrapped in a player's hide', Greene articulates (again,
inadvertently) a notable preoccupation with concealment in the plays
('tiger's heart' also appears in *Henry VI Part Three* (1.4.138)).[1] Just as
Iago hides his hatred behind false friendship, just as Portia and Imogen
conceal their genders, and just as the four lovers of *Love's Labour's Lost*
mask their identities for gags, so too does Shakespeare appear to conceal
his own identity throughout the course of his career, preferring instead
to produce works that championed the malleability of the 'player's hide'
instead of the biography behind the authorial craft (see also Wells 1995:
14–15).

The persistent possibility within the plays for concealment and malleability is arguably one of the reasons why Shakespearean cinema is as successful and prolific at the beginning of its second century, and almost four
hundred years after the death of William Shakespeare. Like their author,
the plays' performative 'identity' is fluid and unfixed. Few stage directions
throughout the original texts grant contemporary directors and actors freedom to inject their own ideas for performance into the Shakespearean play.
The plays' themes of love, death, jealousy, friendship, political corruption
and cultural divisions are at the heart of social dynamics, regardless of
historical or geographical position. Plays such as *Henry V* and *Richard III*,
for example, centralise three-dimensional political tyrants within a (somewhat) historically specific framework, yet have been employed by filmmakers to comment upon similar figures and themes of the twentieth century,
such as Richard Loncraine's commentary on the Nazi regime in his *Richard
III* (1995), and Kenneth Branagh's grim post-Falklands War rendition of
Henry V (1989), in stark contrast to Laurence Olivier's 1944 version of the
same play which asserted its efforts to rouse patriotism during World War

II. For better or for worse, it seems, the Shakespearean 'hide' can serve successfully as political propaganda.

More generally, the plays' latent refusal to stay in one setting, genre, language, nation, character-position or historical juncture is one reason why Shakespeare continues to be popular. In the twenty-first century, cultural activity with the Bard is diverse, and the current 'trend' is to re-work Shakespeare for screen as imaginatively and as contemporaneously as possible: for instance, Katherine Minola (*The Taming of the Shrew*) as a candidate for British Prime Minister; Richard III as a drug-selling 'street king' in east LA; both *Macbeth* and *A Midsummer Night's Dream* set in a rave; *Macbeth* in an up-market London restaurant, run-down US diner, and Mumbai Mafia; *Much Ado About Nothing* in a television studio; and Hamlet as an avid filmmaker in millennial New York.

These 'rare visions', as Puck suggested, have offended scholars and viewers across the globe. The lack of Shakespearean language in some and the re-organisation (or virtual absence) of the Shakespearean text in many productions continue to cause debate as to what actually constitutes a Shakespeare film. Is the title alone sufficient to deem a film worthy of the Bard's name? Is updating Shakespeare's language enough to call a film 'unfaithful'? Must a director include *all* of Shakespeare's lines (as did Kenneth Branagh in his four-hour epic *Hamlet* in 1996), or can these be trimmed down to fit the 'two hours' traffic' of contemporary film? What, in short, makes a film suitable for the cultural paradigm that is Shakespeare?

Whilst a simple answer to this query would undoubtedly satisfy a host of critics, the diversity of Shakespearean cinema is fundamental to its nature. As the following chapters show, progressive, unfaithful Shakespeare films have resulted in emergent adaptational strategies and discourses, while productions which unmoor Shakespeare from his linguistic and cultural posts often articulate cultural identities and anxieties, or contextually highlight problems that are pertinent to a particular social or ethnic group – such as the problems facing LA teens as presented in *The Street King* (2002). When one studies Shakespeare on film, one encounters a *mélange* of social topics that do not solve the mystery of who or what Shakespeare was, is, or will be, but instead enable the student to access those rigorously important dimensions and intersections of cinema, performance and popular culture.

Banking on the Bard

This is not to say, however, that Shakespeare has always brought box-office business. Although Herbert Beerbohm Tree's 'film' of *King John* (1899) was followed by an onslaught of silent Shakespeare productions in cinema's early years, Shakespearean cinema was dogged by the ghost of the theatre and by a paltry box office for most of the twentieth century. In 1989, Kenneth Branagh drew upon his successful stage performance of *Henry V* in his cinematic production of the play. Branagh's film was a box-office hit, garnering two Academy Award nominations and $10 million at the US box office.[2] Perhaps more importantly, however, the film pointedly operated within the generic arena of a host of mainstream war films during the decade, contriving parallels with *Platoon* (1986), *Full Metal Jacket* (1987), and even *Star Wars* (1977) to make its mark on the map of popular culture, and to make the Bard, at last, bankable.

Subsequent films took up Branagh's cue and began tapping into the popular vein, often employing divergent intertextual methods to 'relate' Shakespeare to a cine-literate audience. Franco Zeffirelli's *Hamlet* (1990), for example, thoughtfully cast Mel Gibson – who had recently starred as a suicidal and vengeful cop in the *Mad Max* trilogy (1979, 1981, 1985) and *Lethal Weapon* (1987) – as a suicidal and vengeful Dane, fostering incestuous relations with Glenn Close as his mother Gertrude, who in turn was fresh from her role as a bunny-boiling sexual libertine in *Fatal Attraction* (1987). Baz Luhrmann's *William Shakespeare's Romeo + Juliet* (1996) plugged into MTV culture by employing a gun-fire editing process, rapid zooms, captions, a contemporary soundtrack and rising teen stars (Leonardo DiCaprio and Claire Danes) as the titular lovers. The world of Luhrmann's production is famously, and symbolically, the world of the decaying theatre, suggested by the crumbling theatre structure on Verona Beach and by the replacement of theatricality with metacinema infused with dizzying operatic gestures and characters in drag. Moreover, fragments of other Shakespeare plays, such as *The Tempest* and *Macbeth*, find their way into this film as billboard signs. Symbols replace the text and dominate as sources of meaning. Shakespeare-as-sign in Luhrmann's film was acclaimed not only by audiences and assimilated by subsequent filmmakers, but was additionally applauded by studio bosses as Shakespeare became increasingly synonymous with the sign of the American dollar.

Perhaps the greatest culmination of these mainstream approaches to filming Shakespeare is marked by the Academy Award success of John Madden's *Shakespeare in Love* (1998). Despite studio boss Harvey Weinstein's misgivings about the bankability of Shakespeare – fretting that the appearance of 'Shakespeare' in the film's title would turn away cinema audiences – the film received over US $100 million at the US box office and seven Academy Awards, an accolade for Shakespearean cinema that has yet to be matched.[3]

Notably, the question of Shakespearean authorship permeates *Shakespeare in Love*. An opening scene shows William Shakespeare (Joseph Fiennes) struggling to write a play for which he is commissioned. As he writes, the famous Bardic scrawl carves the film's title letter by letter on-screen, registering the process of Shakespearean screenwriting and ostensibly enforcing the importance of the authentic text. Yet the film goes on to posit Shakespeare's craft as resolutely collaborative, and shows the Renaissance author to be of little importance. The Shakespearean text is attributed to a cacophony of extratextual sources, ranging from Viola (Gwyneth Paltrow) – whom the film imagines as inspiration for the character Juliet – to a street preacher (uttering Mercutio's line, 'a plague on both your houses!'). Christopher 'Kit' Marlowe (Rupert Everett) is figured as a superior playwright and clearly not the author of Shakespeare's plays, yet Shakespeare quickly gives credit where credit seems to be due: 'Marlowe's touch was in my *Titus Andronicus* and my *Henry VI* was a house built on his foundations' (as spoken by Joseph Fiennes as Shakespeare in Madden's film). Shakespeare's 'bankability' in this production is founded on the notion that the Shakespearean text is a permeable chain of voices, signifiers and cultural networks, available for constant re-collaboration and reiteration. The Shakespearean signature appears as an important marker of screen authenticity and legitimacy, yet the authority of the author is reconfigured by cinema's latent intertextual and collaborative logic.

Subsequent films have fared both poorly and well at the box office. After the success of *Much Ado About Nothing* (1993), Branagh's fourth Shakespeare endeavour, the ill-conceived 1930s' Hollywood musical rendition of *Love's Labour's Lost* (2000), reaped a fraction of its US $4 million budget and failed to impress critics around the globe.[4] *10 Things I Hate About You* (1999), Gil Junger's high-school adaptation of *The Taming of the Shrew*, took over US $38 million, yet star-studded productions such as *A Midsummer Night's Dream* (1999) and *The Merchant of Venice* (2004) barely broke even. The issue, it seems, is not simply the presence of Shakespeare, but the performance of Shakespeare according to the evolving performative dynamics of cinema and concerns of popular culture. Chapter 1 therefore examines performance in the context of acting by looking to the most filmed of Shakespeare's plays, *Hamlet*. By examining Svend Gade and Heinz Schall's 1920 version of the play, Laurence Olivier's psychoanalytically-rendered Hamlet of 1948, Grigori Kozintsev's political *Hamlet* of 1964, Kenneth Branagh's macho Dane in his 1996 epic and Franco Zeffirelli's 'populist' *Hamlet* of 1990, the chapter draws attention to the cultural, aesthetic, historical and interpretive ramifications of performance. As this chapter shows, screen performances enliven Shakespeare's plays by interacting with previous performances and the rudiments of the film medium. The performer is shown to act as an interpretive agent, both facilitating and imposing meanings upon the Shakespearean character and, in turn, the Shakespearean text.

Chapter 2 proceeds from these ideas to consider the adaptation politics of Shakespeare on film. Peter Greenaway's *Prospero's Books* (1991) and Kristian Levring's *The King Is Alive* (2001) serve here to demonstrate some of the issues arising from adaptation, such as textuality, 'originality' and authorship. Both films meditate upon the hybrid nature of adaptation, which involves the conflation – and sometimes conflict – of a number of texts and authors, making it difficult to identify both the 'original' and the 'author'. Thrown into disarray in both films, these terms are recognised here as inherently problematic and subject to change. *The King Is Alive* treats *King Lear*'s themes of usurpation and death as correspondent to issues of authorship, whereas *Prospero's Books* imagines authorial power as an 'originating' force, bringing to life textual creations that actually already existed elsewhere. The persistent juxtaposition in both productions of 'original' and 'derivative' offers a convincing analysis of the complexities of adaptation, reminding the viewer that the Shakespearean text is never a singular entity available for re-imagination, but is both a derivative of previous texts and an originating body that circulates amongst numerous derivatives, off-shoots and cultural appropriations.

Chapter 3 looks to style in Shakespearean cinema, with a view to enabling students to 'read' Shakespeare on film. Drawing upon knowledge gained throughout chapters 1 and 2, this chapter accounts for the cinematic rendering of the Shakespeare text. The chapter briefly outlines the dimensions of film style and provides textual and filmic examples, which are further discussed and compared in terms of how these films aesthetically capture Shakespeare's plays. Examples include cinematography in Luhrmann's *Romeo + Juliet*, *mise-en-scène* in Orson Welles' *The Tragedy of Othello: The Moor of Venice* (1952), editing in Akira Kurosawa's *Throne of Blood* (1957) and Michael Almereyda's *Hamlet* (2000) and sound in Richard Loncraine's *Richard III* (1995). Each of these elements of film style is regarded as contributing enormously to the construction and subsequent interpretation of Shakespeare's text. Like performance, film style is determined by a number of industrial, economic, technological and historical factors, each of which are considered in this chapter.

Chapter 4 departs from the concerns raised throughout the preceding three chapters to examine the popularisation of Shakespeare. This is achieved primarily by looking to Shakespeare films that deny a 'faithful' approach to the text, but which raise important social issues and portray ethnic, cultural and sexual identities that have previously been denied representation in Shakespearean cinema. Yet this level of cultural activity has been argued to occur at the cost of the Shakespearean text, which is regarded as gradually 'dumbing down' in twenty-first century cinema. The authenticity of Shakespeare is seen to be amiss, while claims for a multinational or global Shakespeare – refuting the notion of an 'English Bard' – suggest the effects of popularisation as creating a Bard that is not for an age, but for all nations. More generally, these films take up the questions raised in chapter two, forcing us to ask 'Is it Shakespeare?' when mere traces of the Bard can be found in these productions. By considering these issues in *Scotland, PA* (2001) and *O* (2001), the role of Shakespeare on film in popular culture is regarded primarily as enlivening the Shakespeare text from a variety of perspectives.

Whereas a host of texts which conduct a primarily historical approach to Shakespeare on film are already available to the student, this book seeks to situate Shakespeare films in four major critical contexts, as indicated by the previous chapter summary. The films selected are therefore intended to represent and illuminate these contexts. Although each film is considered according to its historical position (such as the factors influencing its production), I deliberately eschew an additional timeline of Shakespearean cinema in order to provide the student with an introductory consideration of theoretical frameworks through which subsequent – or indeed earlier – films may be enjoyed.

A further preoccupation of this book is the relationships between Shakespeare, globalisation and a horizontally-integrated Hollywood at the current moment. Shakespeare, like many global conglomerates and franchises in operation, has become a 'cultural experience'. In much the same way as one can enjoy McDonald's in Turkey, Japan, Rome and Mexico – participating in a similar 'cultural experience' practically anywhere in the world – so too does Shakespeare operate as a sign of predictability and reassurance within a corner of the film market. One knows what to expect at McDonald's, wherever the location. With Shakespeare, there is a similar sense of predictability that far-flung productions have begun to trade upon. At the same time, however, this strident conventionality is undercut by radical methods of appropriating Shakespeare, as though the effort to be 'original' is premised upon postmodern configurations of revision and re-articulation. Yet the problem of originality is, as I have suggested, embedded within the Shakespearean text. Studying Shakespeare on film brings the student to a crevice between old and new texts, old and new performance strategies and technologies, and old and new reception practices.

1   PERFORMANCE

This chapter considers the importance of performance in studying Shakespeare on film. Used here to discuss modes of film acting, performance can also refer to performance numbers in musicals, the way a film 'performs' at the box office, performing the text as an adaptational process, and screening as performance (see also Maltby 2003: 368–72). An actor's performance involves the artificial construction of a character from a series of mannerisms, gestures, physical and vocal characteristics, props, the star persona of the actor and acting methods. Employed across a number of disciplines to discuss a subject's assimilation of a social environment, performance also corresponds with imitation, representation, impersonation, personification, audience dynamics, identification and subjectivity. We shall examine four film performances of *Hamlet* to show the different ways in which performance and its related contexts not only redefine a character and impose meaning on the narrative, but additionally create a host of political, generic, historical, intertextual, ideological and stylistic perspectives through which to reconsider the Shakespearean text.

One of the ways in which this is achieved is performance style. As the following examples demonstrate, acting methods vary considerably across the twentieth century, ranging from the naturalistic Stanislavsky method which proposed realism – or more exactly spontaneity, improvisation and authenticity – as the definitive performative approach to numerous modes of impersonation, presentation and identification. Other schools of performance, such as 'Method' acting, drew upon Stanislavsky's approach to define a rigorously introspective acting style by which the performer 'becomes' the character through psychological and sometimes physical exercises. Influential German dramatist Bertolt Brecht (1898–1956) composed a theory of narrational acting styles, commonly referred to as the Brechtian method or 'acting in quotation marks', by which the performer developed ways of explaining the psychological states of a character rather than seek to impersonate the character. This method of explaining is both subjective and objective, creating a 'contradictory personage, at once Hamlet and a critical witness of Hamlet, the present quoting and the past quoted, simultaneously expressing the sentiments of his role and his own' (Esslin 1971: 137; see also Weideli 1963: 73). In turn, the character is accounted for without emotional appeal, creating a distancing effect from the audience: as though they were scrutinising a psychological profile. In contradistinction to this approach is Murray Smith's study of character engagement which notes the processes of identification inherent in performance as based on emotional cues and responses. Smith's study underscores the way in which performers create a system of identification – a shared point of view – with an audience, a 'structure of sympathy' by which 'particular values, practices, and ideologies' are communicated (1995: 5, 4). Although audience reception and spectatorship are a vital area of performance, this chapter focuses instead on constructions of Hamlet to demonstrate the network of larger cultural and socio-political issues and assumptions which arises from the re-performance of this Shakespearean character.

Nonetheless, it is important to note that performance is inseparable from the narration and often the reception of a film. As an example, the appearance of a particular star in a film can raise our expectations about the film's genre and value. Film posters often feature large images of the film's star(s), indicating 'the star's performance as a separable element of the movie's aggregate package of potential pleasures, one that the audience [may] enjoy as a production value independently of the rest of the movie' (Maltby 2003: 145). The star-as-pleasure-vehicle underscores the process of wish-fulfilment and fantasy that occurs in spectatorship, but also indicates the performer as a symbol of particular cultural values. Christine Geraghty (2000) notes the 'star-as-performer' as a dual persona whose celebrity persona exerts an enormous amount of influence upon performances and upon our expectations and readings of a film. This duality inherent in the star persona is also created by the star's performance in other productions, which generates intertextual dialogues and meanings between films. Mel Gibson's performance as Hamlet in Franco Zeffirelli's film version of the play invokes his previous leading roles in the *Mad Max* trilogy and the *Lethal Weapon* films (1987, 1989, 1992, 1998) bringing to our interpretation of *Hamlet* a host of meanings and definitions that are mediated through these previous performances. According to Richard Dyer, the presence of the star in any production signifies not only the personas that s/he has previously performed, but the image of the star in circulation throughout popular culture (1987: 3). The diversity of ideological and popular discourses that permeate the 'sign' of the star corresponds therefore with every performance, and plays a part in mediating the narrative and our responses to it.

It is equally important to identify performance as a single unit of a film's stylistic elements that integrates with the body of the film. A screen performance must work in conjunction with the camera, and requires an actor to be sensitive to camera angles and focal points, such as extreme close-up. In addition, a performance usually corresponds to the genre or even the style of a production – note the parallels between Branagh's 'epic' *Hamlet* and his performance – and may, as in the case of Kozintsev's *Hamlet*, resonate with the particular political and social landscape of its historical moment. Performance is essentially an interaction between people and, in film, between elements of the medium. The construction of a character is, as these case studies demonstrate, the interaction and construction of cultural values and responses.

Shakespeare's *Hamlet* can be viewed as a meditation on the multiple interactions inherent in performance. In his observation of the phenomenon of 'Hamletism' in the nineteenth century, Kenneth Rothwell has pointed out that '*Hamlet* has and continues to serve for filmmakers, stage directors and actors as the cultural pinnacle of performance' (2002: 27). Embedded within Shakespeare's play, and indeed the character of Hamlet, is a multi-layered portrait of performance, surrounded by the concomitant concerns of deception versus honesty, actor versus audience (or 'observed' versus 'observer' (3.1.153)) and performance versus reality. Shakespeare's play has also been discussed in terms of the 'doubling' that occurs in the context of performance, and it is notable that a similar logic operates within some of the play's recent filmic incarnations (see Lehmann & Starks 2000). In two of the films considered here, the director also plays the leading role. It is therefore important to perceive the 'doubling' of the performer that occurs in the event of the director/actor, as well as the implicit directorial signature inscribed upon the performance.

The subsequent two films examined in this chapter use the play to register important historical and cultural issues, again through a conceptual performative structure. Kozintsev's *Hamlet*, in which Innokenti Smoktunovsky takes the title role, contends with Russia's culturally suffocating political landscape. Smoktunovsky's performance of a heroic Hamlet revolting against a murderous dictator in the form of Claudius lends itself perfectly to the film's political undertones. On the other hand, Zeffirelli's *Hamlet* deliberately contrives a 'Hollywoodised' Prince of Denmark by tapping into the intertextual potency of its star performers and the meanings that their previous roles assign to the film.

Unfortunately, it would be impossible here, and rather superfluous, to examine every filmed *Hamlet* in existence, yet this chapter draws attention to several other versions of *Hamlet* which permit the conceptual value of performance to be appreciated at length. Performances of Ophelia and Gertrude are also analysed, with a view to exploring the ways in which these subordinate characters are played in congruence with or in contrast to the performance of Hamlet. Whereas Hamlet recurrently speaks his mind on a number of topics – providing performers with ample psychological material with which to construct his character – the play's main female characters are, on many occasions, left silent as to their thoughts, feelings and motivations. Did Gertrude cuckold her husband? Did she have a hand in his death? Why did she marry her brother-in-law, Claudius, so soon after Old Hamlet's death? Likewise, what kind of relationship did Ophelia enjoy with Hamlet? What really provokes her madness? Why does she commit suicide? Each of these questions remains gapingly open to interpretation by actors. The performative answers offered within the following case studies illuminate not so much Shakespeare's text, but the ideological force behind the film as a whole. Indeed, a study of the film performances of Ophelia and Gertrude provides us with a significant understanding of filmic constructions of gender across the twentieth century, as well as a consideration of performance in terms of the relationships within the play.

Hamlet: Vacillator? Actor? Female? Freudian subject?

The character of Hamlet is one of the most debated figures in the history of drama. His introspective and mysterious character has been invoked throughout the ages by poets, dramatists, authors and philosophers as a synonym for hesitation, introspection and inner conflict. In the early twentieth century, T. S. Eliot defined a fictional character antithetically in his famous poem, 'The Love Song of J. Alfred Prufrock' (1917):

> No! I am not Prince Hamlet, nor was meant to be:
> Am an attendant lord, one that will do
> To swell a progress, start a scene or two,
> Advise the prince; no doubt, an easy tool,
> Deferential, glad to be of use,
> Politic, cautious, and meticulous;
> Full of high sentence, but a bit obtuse;
> At times, indeed, almost ridiculous –
> Almost, at times, the Fool. (Eliot 1996: 1230)

The character of Prufrock – never named as such throughout the poem – contrasts himself against Hamlet while fretting about his innate indecisiveness. As a character shadowed by 'the pale cast of thought' (3.1.87) to the detriment of his ability to take action, Hamlet's presence in Prufrock's 'love song' ironically underscores Prufrock's vacillation and, as such, contextualises the modern subject as an impotent character. Before Eliot's poem came into existence, however, the character of Hamlet served as the informing study of Sigmund Freud's famous conception of the Oedipus complex. Commencing roughly around the same time as cinema's inception in 1895, Freud's Oedipal theories drew upon Hamlet's melancholic disposition ('I have of late ... lost all my mirth' (2.2.287–8)), the repressed manifestation of his ghostly father and the urgent contemplation throughout the play as characterising features of the Oedipal subject (see Freud 1959).

Freud's reading of Hamlet has informed many filmic interpretations of the play in diverse ways: Olivier's version utilises suggestive camerawork and performances in its heavy portrait of *Hamlet* as a psychoanalytic text; Branagh's Oedipal relationship with his Shakespearean 'father', Derek

Jacobi, is signalled in his production by their matching bleached-blond hairstyles. Mel Gibson's performance as a dagger-drawn Dane holds no punches in its evocation of Hamlet's phallic proclivity and sexual desire for his mother. And, as *Hamlet* provided the basis for one of modernity's defining theoretical principles that in turn corresponded with cinema as a technological representation of the psyche, it is notable that Michael Almereyda's *Hamlet* explores the relationship between *Hamlet* and cinema that was first established in Freudian thought. Ethan Hawke plays Hamlet as a young pensive filmmaker who inhabits Hotel Elsinore, the headquarters of the Denmark Corporation, which is implied as a film company by its logo of a camera shutter and in-house cinema. As we shall examine in chapter 3, Almereyda's film portrays the Prince as a 'maker of (filmic) manners', at once imprisoned by Denmark's surveillance culture and compelled to remember his father by the technologies of memory at his disposal.

This variety of performative interpretations accorded to the Dane seems to suggest the common practice of employing Hamlet as the embodiment of culturally, historically or even subjectively specific characteristics. Freud, for instance, projected his own psyche upon that of Hamlet in his iteration of the Prince's Oedipal complex. As influential Polish critic Jan Kott put it, Hamlet is a 'sponge' who absorbs 'all the problems of our time' (1967: 13). Hamlet's apparent 'universality' is arguably predicated upon the deliberate flexibility of his character and, perhaps more importantly, is enabled by his own questioning of the boundary between performing and 'being'. Hamlet freely puts on an antic disposition, moving between roles as a madman, hero, lover, vengeful heir and play director. He is, in short, the quintessential performer. The act of performing Hamlet gives rise to the question of performing. The play-within-the-play, or Hamlet's 'Mousetrap', designed to trap the King by pricking his guilty conscience, is indicative of the play's *mise-en-abymic* treatment of performance. At almost every level of the play, there is a performance matched by the struggle to define what is real.

This struggle takes various guises throughout the canon of filmed versions of *Hamlet*. A 1907 film, directed and performed by the so-called 'father' of film narrative, Georges Méliès, is recounted by Méliès' brother Gaston as containing a scene in which the director endeavours to portray cinematically Hamlet's conflict with the division of reality and fantasy: 'He is seen in his room where he is continually annoyed and excited by apparitions which taunt him in their weirdness and add bitterness to his troubled brain. He attempts to grasp them but in vain, and he falls to brooding' (quoted in Ball 1968: 34). Famous for his interest in and filmic portraits of spectres and phantoms, Méliès adds another ghost to this production: the ghost of Ophelia, whom Hamlet 'attempts to embrace [but] when he sees the apparition fall to the ground, he too swoons away, and is thus found by several courtiers. He is raving mad and storms about in a manner entirely unintelligible to them' (quoted in Ball 1968: 29). From Méliès' account, Hamlet is tortured by ghostly visitations and, more exactly, by his inability to discern between (corpo)reality and the spectral 'coinages' of his brain.

Svend Gade and Heinz Schall's 1920 version ups the stakes by claiming that Hamlet was a woman. Gade's *Hamlet: A Drama of Vengeance* takes its cue from a nineteenth-century text, Edward Vining's *The Mystery of Hamlet: An Attempt to Solve an Old Problem* (1881), which argued that Hamlet was a woman whose identity had to be concealed so that Denmark would have a male heir to the throne. The film starred Gade's then-wife, the androgynous and proto-feminist Asta Nielsen – a star so famous she was offered, and refused, her own studio in Nazi Germany. The added twist to this production is the suggestion of Hamlet's unrequited passion for Horatio who, running his hand across his dead companion's chest, apparently realises the truth, but too late. Hamlet's enigma is contrived as a somewhat unbelievable sexual masquerade that is intended to register the cruelty of a monarchy that forced Hamlet to perform an alternative gender identity. Though the film pitches its 'take' on *Hamlet* in a deliberately controversial fashion, the notion of performance in Shakespeare's play serves to highlight gender roles and performances at a seminal juncture in the history of feminism.

Throughout the course of the twentieth century *Hamlet* on film is continually reinvented as at the crossroads of a performance-related crisis. The various dimensions throughout Shakespeare's play configure performance conceptually as congruent with four major factors: place, psychological profile, narrative and production style/format. We shall examine the following case studies with these contexts in mind.

The man who couldn't make up his mind

Following the success of his début film, *Henry V*, Laurence Olivier produced a second directorial effort in the form of his 1948 version of *Hamlet*, during which he was knighted for his services to the theatre. Olivier had previously performed an unabridged version of *Hamlet* on stage in 1937, and rose to international acclaim as the lead in Samuel Goldwyn's film version of *Wuthering Heights* (1939). His renowned psychoanalytic rendering of the Dane took up, somewhat naïvely, Dr Ernest Jones' post-Freudian thesis of Hamlet as a repressed Oedipus to construct a 'vaginally hooded' marital bed in the midst of a maze-like Elsinore (Donaldson 1990: 31). Critics have since departed from the film's explicitly psychoanalytic meditations to consider the imprint of Olivier's own subconscious upon the production, particularly the film's preoccupation with stairs. In his autobiography, Olivier recounted an attempted rape that happened on the stairs of his boarding school at nine years old (1982: 18–19). Ostensibly recalling this event, the stairs in Olivier's *Hamlet* can be read as signalling perverse and non-consensual sex. The film's physical space echoes the obviously theatrical setting of Olivier's *Henry V*, which opens with the Chorus' rendition of the prologue on stage. In *Hamlet*, however, space is markedly and cinematically symbolic. Elsinore's pillars – emblematic of phallic dominance – correspond with the symbolic function of the stairs and, to an equal extent, the castle's long, arched corridors, which reflect the shape of the marital bed. In a psychoanalytic reading, the castle imprisons its inhabitants within the 'incestuous sheets' (1.2.157) of Gertrude and Claudius' union.

Although *Henry V* was shot in colour, Olivier presents *Hamlet* in black and white. This is possibly to avail of the expressive potency of chiaroscuro, and arguably to draw comparisons between contemporary director Alfred Hitchcock's psychoanalytic aesthetic, as evidenced by *Spellbound* (1945) and *Notorious* (1946). At the outset, Olivier adds his own dialogue, telling us that 'this is the tragedy of a man who could not make up his mind'. Later, Olivier would comment that the film was to be regarded as an 'essay' on the play, instead of a representation. Yet the film neither realises Olivier's intended 'thesis', nor does it satisfy as a visual essay. Its most arresting quality lies in the Hitchcock-inspired associations between performers and architecture framed by an explicit interest in the subconscious.

Olivier frequently bookends scenes with dizzying shots of Elsinore's symbolic interiors, and his 'To be or not to be' scene is no different. Shifting the scene *after* Hamlet's confrontation with Ophelia ('it hath made me mad' (3.1.146)), Olivier's camera pulls away from a sobbing, prostrate

Ophelia, moving backwards up the stairs. Soaring up six or seven flights, the camera finally arcs towards the sky before lowering to the sea at the foot of the castle walls. Here we share Hamlet's point of view. The back of his head comes into shot as he peers down at the waves. Moving towards and 'inside' Hamlet's head, we hear the words 'to be or not to be, that is the question' whilst a series of slow superimpositions show the lapping tide soothingly 'rubbing' Hamlet's furrowed brow, thus furnishing Hamlet's 'sea of troubles' (3.1.61) with a visual reference. Olivier makes no bones about the fact that this scene is a suicide attempt, or rather a languid contemplation of suicide that is reneged at the line 'fly to others that we know not of' (3.1.84). Shakespeare's soliloquy operates here as a cross between inner monologue and solo performance. Swooning on a rock at the cliff-edge, Olivier holds a dagger at his chest as the words 'to die, to sleep' enter his consciousness. Thereafter, the camera stays static, framing Olivier in a mid-shot on the rock, until he inadvertently drops the dagger into the sea and saunters off into the mists at the line 'lose the name of action'. Some have argued for the dropped dagger as representative of castration, suggesting the entirety of the scene – and the interpretation of 'to be or not to be' – as a repressed desire to re-enter the maternal womb (Donaldson 1990: 31). It is important to note, however, that Olivier's performance works in co-operation with suggestive props, architecture and cinematography to generate such interpretations, and is stylistically never emblematic in itself. Orchestrated according to the film's prescribed theoretical approach, Olivier's languid performance is in keeping with the rudiments of melodrama. As Andrew Klevan observes, melodramatic performances relieve 'the performer of the need to overtly or openly express their psychological states and betray their latent or covert aspects' for the reason that 'other aspects of a film's presentation' operate as expressive, or external forces, of a character's psychology (2005: 14). In short, Olivier's performance is one component of a larger, integral whole.

Ophelia here is played by 18-year-old Jean Simmons. With bleached blonde tresses and white flowery frocks, Simmons presents a virginal, hysterical Ophelia who obeys her father and brother and is consistently sweet. She is figured as a character that does not succumb to madness, but instead regresses to an infantile psychological state as a result of a desire, like Hamlet, to return to the womb. This is configured by her melodramatic performance in tandem with architectural framing. Towards the end of the scene in which Polonius counsels Laertes 'to thine own self be true', once Polonius has told her not 'to give words or talk to the Lord Hamlet' (1.3.134), she looks down a long arched corridor at Hamlet, who appears diminutively in a room at the bottom. A subsequent shot shows Hamlet looking back at her through the arches as he lounges in what looks like a director's chair. The long, arched passageway that links the two figures – already matched by their similar hair colour – is, in conjunction with the significance of the marital bed, evocative of a birth canal. The relationship between Hamlet and Ophelia is marked therefore not by romantic inclinations, but by a joint effort to fulfil the desires of the subconscious.

The scenes preceding Ophelia's suicide show a reprisal of her framing under the arches. Appearing unhinged and very bridal, Ophelia runs from a pond outside the castle to a courtyard inside where she is met by Gertrude and Claudius. Here Ophelia is not so much grief-stricken but in the throes of a performance as the classical madwoman, wailing and singing nonsense even as she floats to her death down the river. Simmons' performance seems deliberately to eschew sympathy for or understanding of her character; instead, we are called upon to understand the way in which Ophelia functions to symbolise, or articulate, the film's theoretical investments. More telling in this regard is a previous shot of Ophelia exiting the castle towards the river through a long arched corridor. Framed once again by an increasingly symbolic motif, Ophelia is the subject of Olivier's painting; her subjectivity, played out according to a Freudian theme, is never revealed.

Olivier's direction solicits strong performances in accordance with the styles of the era, but filters these performances – including his own – through a meticulously controlled theoretical 'lens'. Moreover, each of the performances participates in the construction of an imposed interpretation of Hamlet's character, resulting in performances that deliberately avoid developing autonomous characters to create personas that are defined by their relationship to Hamlet's world and, indeed, his indecisive psyche.

The 'Banned' Bard

Olivier's depiction of an indecisive Dane corresponded with *Hamlet*'s troubled history with the former Soviet Union. Josef Stalin famously claimed that 'Hamlet's indecisiveness and depression are incompatible with the new Soviet spirit of optimism, fortitude, and clarity', resulting in a virtual cessation of Hamlet performances during Stalin's regime (see Epstein 1993: 353). Yet Stalin's influential condemnation of the play – which was followed by only 14 Soviet productions of Hamlet from 1945 and 1957 in contrast with 78 of Othello – was more than a personal dislike for Hamlet's character (Chura 2000). The play's oppressive social milieu and the portrait of a tyrannical, murderous king resonated with Stalin's reign of terror, while the play's layers of social criticism and ideologies of resistance were deemed 'unsuitable' for the Soviet population. As Marxist theatre and film director Grigori Kozintsev put it, 'Hamlet thinks ... There is nothing more dangerous' (1966: 250).

Kozintsev's film version of Hamlet came ten years after his post-Stalin stage version at the Leningrad Pushkin Theatre, which, featuring the music of Dmitri Shostakovich and produced within a year of Stalin's death, was marked as an artistic retaliation against three decades of cultural repression. Kozintsev's Hamlet of 1964, based on a translation of the play by Boris Pasternak, marked additional political contexts: Stalin's successor, Nikita Kruschev, was outspoken about the 'cult of personality' that pervaded Stalin's rule and promoted some successful counter-reforms throughout the Soviet Union. In the year of the film's release, Kruschev's former protégé, Leonid Brezhnev, successfully ousted and replaced Kruschev as the leader of the Soviet Union. It was not long before Kruschev's anti-Stalin policies were crushed, resulting in an alarming regression to the stifling bureaucracy and persecution that had plagued the Soviet Union for most of the twentieth century. Accordingly, the reprise of a bleak social outlook is reflected in Kozintsev's portrait of Denmark's turbulent sea, broken crosses (which resemble axes), downtrodden peasantry and close-ups of the jaw-like portcullis of Elsinore's drawbridge closing around its inhabitants and the film's spectators as it moves threateningly from the top to the bottom of the frame. The wheel that the peasants push at the beginning to close the drawbridge evokes the wheel of history, returning the denizens of Denmark to a despotic past and closing the drawbridge on the castle of oppression.

It is fitting, therefore, that Kozintsev's Marxist Dane should be played by Innokenti Smoktunovsky, a rising Soviet star and former Nazi POW who served in the Russian Red Army. Smoktunovsky's Hamlet is not an idle thinker, nor is he prone to hesitation. He is an openly rebellious figure of resistance who martyrs himself in the pursuit of democracy. Smoktunovsky was almost forty years old when he took up the role – marginally younger than Olivier – yet his performance retains the quiet poise and youthful dynamism that is clearly intended here to characterise the Dane. This Hamlet's turmoil is not psychological; it is clearly caused by his inhabitation of a politically corrupt environment, and his knowledge that *he alone* must bring the criminal monarchy to its knees.

Kozintsev's cinematography is consistently, and poetically, political. In order to enforce Hamlet's conception of Denmark as 'a prison' (2.2.239), for instance, Kozintsev recurrently shoots his actors behind bar-like objects. The 'get thee to a nunnery' scene (3.1.122) is particularly striking in this regard. Ophelia, portrayed by Anastasiya Vertinskaya as a delicate puppet, is sent in as bait for Hamlet whilst Polonius (Yuri Tolubeyev) and Claudius (Mikhail Nazvanov) hide in an adjacent corridor. She enters from beneath a large staircase that Hamlet descends. He is shown behind the wooden banister pillars as if imprisoned; likewise, shots cutting back to Ophelia show her looking up at him – as Hamlet looked up earlier at the monstrous ghost of Old Hamlet – and convey her as 'trapped' behind the staircase. The suggestion at this point is that Claudius' and Polonius' plot to spy on Hamlet and Ophelia is trapping them within a politically-structured 'web' that will eventually bring about their deaths. Hamlet's advice to Ophelia to 'get thee to a nunnery' is accordingly marked not with disdain, but with solemn undertones of the patriarchal prison in which she is becoming incarcerated, and should therefore flee. A later shot of Ophelia in an iron corset in preparation for her father's funeral reinforces the sense of her imprisonment, and proffers her subsequent death as a noble attempt at freedom. A shot of Ophelia's dead body underwater is followed by a shot of the castle's reflection. Significantly, Ophelia has finally laid herself to rest beyond the boundaries of that reflection.

Hamlet's dynamism is further indicated by the chamber scene, in which he visits his mother, Gertrude (Elsa Radzina-Szolkonis), and kills Polonius. Hamlet stalks towards his mother's chamber, silencing a guard by placing a hand on his mouth and shoving him backwards without effort. Upon entering the chamber, Smoktunovsky's countenance alone is enough to make Gertrude shriek for help. The ghost's presence is signalled only by Shostakovich's score and by Hamlet's awe-struck glance upward. When

Fig. 1: Innokenti Smoktunovsky as Hamlet, entering the throne room in Kozinstev's *Hamlet* (1964)

Hamlet lugs the guts of Polonius' dead body out of the room, he chuckles. Smoktunovsky's Hamlet is neither mad, nor is he a performer. He is controlled, powerful and merciless. This is confirmed in a subsequent scene when he is made to answer for Polonius' death. Again he walks undeterred to the king, startling a guard when he seizes a torch out of its sheath. He enters the room with the flame held straight out in front of him, a gesture to the Nazi salute. Having seized the courtiers' attention, Hamlet tosses the torch aside. Coolly answering the king's questions, Hamlet reprises his earlier treatment of Ophelia – walking around her in circles, probing her with questions – by silently prowling around the room past each of the courtiers as he eyeballs them, before exiting. Later, when Laertes' poisoned blade brings death to Hamlet, he does not wilt to the floor, but rather walks outside the castle and rests upright against the cliff, looking out to sea. The suggestion is that even in death, he is still standing.

Smoktunovsky's performance contradicts Olivier's rendition by depicting a solid, undeterred political outsider who eventually martyrs himself in the quest for liberty. Smoktunovsky's Hamlet does not interact with an overarching theoretical interpretation, as does Olivier's, but complements Kozintsev's cinematographic interest in imprisonment so as to heighten this character's struggle for freedom. This struggle, in keeping with the political climate of the film's historical moment and geographical specificity, is not for personal liberty, but for social escape from tyrannical oppression. Somewhat in accordance with Stalin's rejection of Hamlet's latent indecisiveness, Hamlet here is the definition of resolve.

The populist performer

Franco Zeffirelli allegedly selected Mel Gibson for the title role in his film *Hamlet* after watching Gibson's suicide scene as widowed cop Martin Riggs in *Lethal Weapon*. The result is a populist *Hamlet* that sponged up the generic proclivity during the 1980s for filmic representations of masculine heroism. A far cry from Olivier's effeminate and indecisive Hamlet, Gibson's performance outlines the Dane as an action hero at odds with his society. Yet, unlike Smoktunovsky's public enemy, Gibson's heroic Hamlet is urged on not by political liberty or grief for his father, but by pent-up passion for his promiscuous mother. Whereas Olivier's psychoanalytic interpretation of the play offered symbolic connotations of Hamlet's sexual inclinations towards his mother, Gibson's Prince provides a garishly explicit depiction of masculine aggressivity that stems not from a repressed subconscious, but from a repressed libido. Gibson's performance achieves this interpretation first and foremost by his constant employment of a symbolic prop: his long, drawn sword. Rarely seen without it, Hamlet clangs his sword off the castle barracks, sending sparks flying into the night. A little later, the sword is out again as he makes Horatio (Stephen Dillane) and his men (Richard Warwick and Christien Anholt) swear not to tell about the visitation. And, when he visits his mother in her chamber, the sword is swung like a baton. These recurrent phallic gestures are present from the outset, when a shot of Gertrude leaning over her late husband's coffin captures the sword placed on the cap stone pointing downwards directly at her. As the common denominator of a sexual triangle, Gertrude is figured clearly in this Hollywood effort as the protagonist's object of desire.

Gibson's performance operates in congruence with Zeffirelli's camerawork and settings. In terms of the former, Zeffirelli continually juxtaposes Gibson cinematographically with subordinate characters in order to empower his character by contrast. For instance, when the ghost of Old Hamlet appears for a second time, the shot cuts not to Hamlet, but first to an anonymous armed guard who leaps backwards in fear. There is a pan right to Hamlet, who shoots forward towards the ghost, shocked but unhesitant. The ghost does not loom upon his audience as did Kozintsev's, but rather plays hide and seek until Hamlet, after fending off his protective friends with his sword, follows the ghost to the top of the castle – again with his sword drawn. Hamlet is thus portrayed as unhesitant, brave and unfailing when others flinch.

Zeffirelli's settings also provide a motivational context for Hamlet's soliloquies, thereby disavowing the latent introspection of the character by connecting his thoughts to external scenes. An example of this is the 'to be or not to be' scene, which takes place underground in the family crypt. Zeffirelli's chosen setting for this scene is crucial in suggesting that Gibson's Hamlet is *not* contemplating suicide, but rather musing upon death as he pays dutiful respects to his ancestors. Surrounded by sarcophagi topped with life-size figurines, Hamlet's meditation on the comparison between death and sleep seems to furnish the entire speech with an outward motivation, substituting the 'pale cast of thought' (3.1.87) with which Hamlet is afflicted – underscored by an overhead beam of light into which Hamlet steps, and his glance upwards – with a heightened resolve to take action. Gibson's performance builds upon Zeffirelli's camerawork and settings to carve a handsome, virile and entertaining Prince whose virtues are in strict opposition to the villain, Claudius (Alan Bates) – who is stereotypically European and overtly lecherous – and whose longing for his mother is to be taken rather sympathetically as a result of unfulfilled masculine desire.

Perhaps to reinforce Hamlet's sexual frustration, his romantic interest in the film is depicted as a virginal, twitchy, naïve teenager, in stark contrast to Close's seductive, brazen, confident Gertrude. Helena Bonham Carter's performance of Ophelia is not entirely convincing: her character does not have much function or importance in the film, leaving Bonham Carter with unspent performative energy that crackles beneath her youthful exterior. Many of her lines are cut and replaced with scenes featuring Hamlet. A striking example of this is Hamlet's post-ghost visit which, in the play, Ophelia recounts to her father. Here, however, Ophelia remains silent and out of frame for the most part, and is moved briefly to tears by Hamlet's desperate appearance. In the 'get thee to a nunnery' scene – which comes across as rather stagy – Ophelia's lines are drastically reduced, leaving her once again merely to react instead of taking any kind of action. Her back is turned to the camera for a frustrating amount of time, until at last she spins away from Hamlet to face the camera. Most of her performance seems preoccupied with such fighting for frame-time. She seems to get her dues upon Polonius' death, when she wanders around the battlements making lewd advances at unsuspecting soldiers, adroitly articulating a sudden barrage of lines and managing the appearance of a damned wretch with skill.

The scene in which Hamlet kills Polonius is of particular importance in facilitating the film's portrait of sexuality. Calling 'mother' from off-screen, Hamlet strides into her chamber moments after Polonius has concealed himself behind a curtain, and swings his sword around. Using it as a walking stick and frequently pointing it at his mother – using it also to force her to sit – Hamlet thrusts his sword through the curtain within seconds of entering the room and kills Polonius. Despite this error, the sword henceforth remains unsheathed. Hamlet chases his mother around the room to see if her heart 'be made of penetrable stuff' (3.4.35), then pushes her onto the bed and, after showing her locket pictures of Claudius and Old Hamlet, uses her own locket to throttle her. The rest of the scene is portrayed as a semi-rape, with Hamlet straddling his mother and thrusting into her while she sobs, rhythmically punctuating his syllables to insinuate penetration: 'but to live/in the rank sweat of an enseaméd bed,/stewed in corruption, honeying and making love' (3.4.81–3). Accordingly, Gertrude's plea to 'speak to me no more' (3.4.84) seems less a request not to hear the truth than to put a stop to the apparent rape. When this does not work, she holds Hamlet in a long, passionate kiss. At this, the ghost appears – ostensibly to prevent incest than to counsel Hamlet – and the pair are broken up. Cupping Gertrude's face, Hamlet urges Gertrude to 'confess yourself to heaven' (3.4.140), before leaving her – with Polonius' dead body in tow – to her thoughts. There is nothing of a mother/son dynamic in either performance, but rather that of an aggressor/victim intimidation that suggests a sexual undercurrent which has reached its apex.

Gibson's performance capitalises on Zeffirelli's 'populist' approach by replacing political circumstance and subconscious rumination with a detailed portrait of post-*Rambo* masculinity. The primary correlations in Gibson's performance are his suggestive prop and Zeffirelli's contextualising settings, yet his performance also echoes his previous performances as Mad Max and Martin Riggs, who are volatile, homicidal, heroic, comic, weapon-wielding characters. Gibson's Hamlet also coheres with a rather classical character-driven narrative, which is arguably a major contribution to the film's success. Thanks to a pruned down, well-spliced script, his character consistently drives the plot forward, taking time to ponder the meaning of death only when it provides the audience with breathing space between action scenes. It is Hamlet's point of view that we share; it is Hamlet who tells the story; and it is Hamlet who resolves the state of crisis that he, in turn, incited at the film's beginning. Gibson's performance is complicit, therefore, with a scrupulously refashioned narrative that places the protagonist, his goal and the outcome in their perfect 'Hollywood' positions.

Hamlet uncut

Kenneth Branagh's version of *Hamlet* is a celebration of the play of deliberately epic proportions, featuring a huge star cast (many of which appear in blink-and-miss cameo roles), dazzling sets, and Shakespeare's text in its entirety, combining the play's academically approved versions, the First Folio and Second Quarto. Alongside a reverence for Shakespeare's poetry are interpolative flashbacks and filmic asides that roll flat any ambiguities within the Shakespearean text. This production was intended to depart from previous populist, political and psychoanalytic versions in order to create the 'definitive' cinematic *Hamlet*: a *Hamlet* for the thinking masses. As Branagh put it,

> We want this *Hamlet* to be a big, big treat. We're trying for a more epic sweep than is usually contemplated ... there will be thousands of extras for some sequences. The Ghost is going to be a lot scarier than some faintly benign old sort walking on stage in a white shirt. It ain't gonna be three-and-a-half hours of talking heads. (Quoted in Arnold 1996: 36–7)

Accordingly, Branagh's performance as Hamlet is larger than life, wholly befitting the film's extravagance. Occupying almost every scene of this four-hour production, Branagh's Hamlet is at times exhausting for both viewer and (presumably) performer. His performance is stimulating, traversing with swift dexterity the broad spans of sullen son, energetic comedian, gleeful friend, venomous ex-lover, talented actor, agile fencer and vociferous contemplator that apparently encompass Hamlet's disposition. Branagh's diction is crisp, musical and sculpted, no doubt, by his previous performances of the play with both his own company – the Renaissance Theatre Company – and the Royal Shakespeare Company. Although his soliloquies often climax to thunderous bawling, Branagh's Hamlet makes for a vigorously dynamic performance that unabashedly aspires to the grandiose. Despite his proclamation that this was to be an 'anti-Oedipal' production of the play, Branagh's performance seems to bear the 'weight of the ghosts of other performances', which he previously described with regards to his earlier performances of Shakespearean characters on-stage (see Crowl 1994: 6). Branagh's performance of the 'to be or not to be' scene serves as a fine example of the anxiety of 'doubling' that, despite all inten-tions, registers Oedipal concerns at the level of performing Hamlet.

In this scene Branagh enters Elsinore's court hall, which is lined at both sides with large double-sided mirrors that both conceal interior rooms and reflect Elsinore's inhabitants. This is one of the film's most self-conscious and cinematic scenes. Branagh's gesture to his filmic forefather, Sir Laurence Olivier, and his theatrical forefather (who previously directed him in a stage version of *Hamlet* and who stars here as Claudius), Derek Jacobi, is evidenced by his peroxide hair, yet this scene shows the 'weight' of these father-figures upon his interpretation of the Dane. Here Branagh faces his reflection in one of the mirrors as he commences the soliloquy, showing 'two' Branaghs at either side of the frame. A reverse-shot shows Polonius (Richard Briers) and Claudius in a room behind the mirror watch-ing on. A long-take focuses on Branagh as he dictates the soliloquy, slowly approaching the mirror and then drawing his dagger at his reflection. Enter Ophelia (Kate Winslet) to return Hamlet's 'remembances'. At first there are traces of the love affair gestured at during previous flashbacks, yet the door to Polonius' room at the end of the long hall is significantly kept, albeit out of focus, in frame between the two, suggestive of his intrusion into their affair. Hamlet hugs and kisses her, but slaps the letters out of her hand when she motions to hand them back. Hamlet's question, 'Where is your father?' is prompted by a sudden noise made by Claudius in the room behind the mirror. Unsatisfied with her retort ('At home, my lord'), Hamlet proceeds to drag Ophelia violently behind him as he opens the doors behind each of the mirrors. Finally, he shoves Ophelia's face against the mirror behind which Claudius and Polonius watch on. A shot from behind

Fig. 2: Kenneth Branagh as Hamlet, confronting his 'double'

the glass shows Hamlet staring at Claudius and Polonius as if he can see them; one is never quite sure whether Hamlet is staring at his reflection or Claudius, and the ambiguity seems intentional.

In many ways Claudius here is Hamlet's reflection, his double, which Hamlet intends to kill. Branagh's film thus reaches for a far more complex psychoanalytic portrait of *Hamlet* than does Olivier's, insofar as Branagh self-consciously explores the 'doubling' effect that occurs in re-making *Hamlet* by gesturing towards previous performances and performers (such as John Gielgud, Olivier and of course Jacobi). In short, Freud's thesis on the 'uncanny' indicates a period of psychological development during which the self may identify too strongly with an 'other', in which case the 'double' self becomes a threat, a 'harbinger of death' (Freud 1995: 235). In Branagh's case, this theoretical principle is played out in terms of Claudius as a psychological projection of Hamlet who threatens Hamlet's identity and, thus, must be killed. Secondly, the two Branaghs that appear in the frame signal the presence of the dual figure of performer and director in this production as a Janus-faced entity. And thirdly, the fact that the mirror 'screens' or conceals Claudius and reflects Hamlet seems to suggest Claudius in this production to some extent as psychologically related to Hamlet. Indeed, the face behind the reflection indicates the circularity of revenge that pervades *Hamlet*, picked up by Branagh in this scene and later on when his attempt to kill Claudius as he prays imagines Hamlet's dagger penetrating Claudius' ear: exactly in the manner in which Claudius killed Old Hamlet. And of course, when Gertrude exclaims that Hamlet's 'words like daggers enter into mine ears' (3.4.85), the pattern seems to continue. And continue it does, until Hamlet's death: Laertes' desire to avenge Polonius' death is exploited by Claudius to wipe Hamlet out. With the exception of Ophelia and Gertrude, all those that sought revenge in the play are shown to come to death.

Kate Winslet's performance as Ophelia is sensitive, complex and timely. Flashbacks of Ophelia and Hamlet in bed give rise to interpretations of her descent from an apparently sturdy emotional state to straitjacketed delirium as motivated in part by a sexual passion gone awry. In one scene Ophelia rushes into Polonius' chamber to tell him of a visit from Hamlet in which he appeared 'as if he had been loosed out of hell/to speak of horrors' (2.1.84–85). Usually this scene is facilitated by a flashback of Hamlet's appearance. But here, Winslet manages to convey the scene all on her own. Sobbing and shaken, Winslet performs Hamlet's actions as she tells them, finally bursting into a seething, tearful fit of frustration at her father for making her 'repel [Hamlet's] letters' and '[denying] him access to me'. Winslet's performance, in tandem with Branagh's decision to forgo the standard flashback, brings attention to the effects of the ghost's visit on Ophelia. In addition, it appears that Ophelia's escalating turmoil is created by blind obedience to Polonius' request that she reject Hamlet: a sympathetic portrait of her frustration at poor paternal counsel. A subsequent scene shows Ophelia presented by her father before the King and Queen (Julie Christie), and forced to read one of Hamlet's love letters. Winslet reads the letter with aching reluctance, trembling and weeping until she is forced to flee the room in tears. Polonius is unmoved by his daughter's grief; Richard Briers' Polonius is selfish, hypocritical, and, as Hamlet says, a 'tedious old fool' (2.2.215), whose treatment of Ophelia is abhorrently selfish. Nonetheless, when Polonius' body is taken for burial, Ophelia screams as she clutches against the iron bars of a locked gate which prevent her from reaching his body – a crafty allusion to Elsinore's imprisonment of affection and love. This is confirmed by a later shot which shows Ophelia – framed again by bars – bashing herself against the adjacent walls of a padded cell.

Both performances go beyond earlier productions of the play to flesh out and update Shakespeare's characters – by showing Ophelia as a passionate victim of patriarchy and political corruption, for instance, instead of a batty maid who melts into watery insanity under Hamlet's blistering rebuttals. At times, however, it seems as though Branagh's 'pendulum' performance – swinging between as many as three emotional states in one scene – verges on inconsistency and, instead of demonstrating the complexity of Hamlet's character, teeters on confusion. When Hamlet kills Polonius, for instance, he does not show a modicum of regret, sorrow or doubt. Instead, the slightly off-kilter entertainer reaches his apex as he jibes with Claudius about the location of the murdered body. Whilst the play lightens the mood of the previous scene by taking Hamlet's wit to a higher level, Branagh's display of arrogant comedy grinds against his character's tender side, as portrayed towards the end of the previous scene with Gertrude. In short, this makes for a challenging performance that nonetheless underscores Hamlet's cultural weight, and articulates the spectral traces inscribed upon each new performance by previous 'ghosts'.

Conclusions

In each of the given examples, performance vitalises *Hamlet* in a variety of culturally specific contexts. Performance can be acknowledged as a vital factor in a film's reception and interpretation, bringing to the character, and the original text in the case of Shakespeare films, numerous intertextual, sexual, political and historical meanings that circulate within society. A performer is a narrational agent; he or she is responsible for the conveyance of the film's narrative. Sometimes narration involves voice-over reportage of the plot, but most often narration is executed alongside point-of-view shots which enable us to identify with or indeed share the protagonist's subjectivity. The way in which an actor narrates or performs the text's 'information' is crucial in determining our interpretation of the character and engagement with the film as a whole.

Performance can be understood as a mode of collaboration between and interaction with other elements of the film, such as location and production sets, cinematography, narrative style and the directorial approach to Shakespeare's text. More importantly, however, is the recognition of the Shakespearean text as a primary source for performance. As Judith Buchanan observes,

> the mutability of a text's meanings in performance ... alerts us to the provisional character of that originating text. It is inherently a document of possibilities that can ambush us anew in performance as its multiple points of collaborative interaction come together in ways not before experienced. (2005: 3)

The text is 'provisional' insofar as its meaning is never fixed. Performance is thus a mediatory action that transmits the text to an audience according to a particular interpretive position. The trajectory of performance in Shakespearean cinema is always towards its source, back to the text through a gamut of previous performative interpretations.

2   ADAPTATION

Georges Méliès' 1907 film, *Le Rêve de Shakespeare* (literally 'the dream of Shakespeare', known in English as *Shakespeare Writing Julius Caesar*), depicts the creation of a Shakespearean play. Showing the Bard struggling to 'devise the scene in which Julius Caesar is murdered by the conspirators', the film finally shows how Shakespeare's 'thoughts take life' and come into existence before him as a performed play (Ball 1968: 35). Méliès-as-Shakespeare is seated to the far right of the frame, watching his conception of Caesar's murder at the top of a small flight of stairs, arm outstretched against the four swords drawn upon him. Once the deed is done, the scene returns to the initial location of Shakespeare's study, and the Bard is shown to be revived from his previous bout of writer's block (see Lanier 2002: 61–2).

Méliès' short film significantly conveys the author as 'fathering-forth' the text as a cinematic entity.[1] The scene of writing is preceded, or perhaps replaced, by the effortless conjuring of a scene that is defined by its filmicity, in which the author, also a spectator and the film's director, is present in the *mise-en-scène*. This triadic formulation of the author is a crucial reflexive element of Méliès' presentation of the author. Alongside the film's portrait of authorial conception is the notion of Shakespeare's craft as a revisionary process, and not an original creation. That is, the subject of both Shakespeare's dream and play is a historical event, recounted in Plutarch's first-century text *Lives of the Noble Greeks and Romans*. The play that is performed before Shakespeare in Méliès' film is therefore not an 'original' manifestation but a dramatisation of history conceived from the Bard's point of view.

Without realising it, Méliès' film presented some of the major issues that would permeate Shakespearean cinema for years to come. The process of adaptation is conveyed in this film as a cinematic mode of conception and birth, providing the immobile texts of history and ancient literature with movement, visuality and corporeality. The author appears as an originating agent, bestowed by the phallic quill with life-giving powers superseding the maternal. Adaptation, this film suggests, is the practice by which such originating capabilities can come into being.

The films examined in this chapter – *Prospero's Books*, an adaptation of *The Tempest; and The King Is Alive*, an adaptation of *King Lear* – present the informing issues and contexts of adaptation in a more complex fashion than Méliès' film in reflection of the complicated relationship between text and screen at the cusp of cinema's second century. Both films question the author's identity, responsibility and legitimacy as a point of origin. Notably, neither film uses the play's original title. Although there may be a number of reasons for this, the common trend in recent Shakespeare films to revise both the plot of a Shakespearean play and its title suggest less a denouncement of the Shakespeare element of a production than an acknowledgement of the textual transpositions with which audiences are acutely familiar. In many ways, Umberto Eco's notion of the 'already said', or the idea of postmodern replication and the crisis of originality informs these productions, which are always in tension with previous films (1994: 68). Added to this crisis is the 'hybrid' nature of adaptation, which ineluctably sets the literary text in conflict with the film text. In representation of these issues, *Prospero's Books* and *The King Is Alive* suitably explore the way in which textual transposition reveals and informs us of the nature of both cinema and the literary text. This chapter therefore considers these films in terms of their diverse portraits of 'textuality', authorship and originality to facilitate a deeper understanding of the role of adaptation in Shakespeare on film, and to prompt consideration of adaptation's informing critical contexts.

Adaptation: definitions and categories

Adaptation is a blanket term for the process by which a text is visualised on screen. Throughout the twentieth century, this term has been frequently broken down into sub-categories by scholars who detect and aim to describe various definitions of the relationship between text and screen, such as Jack Jorgens' 'three degrees of distance' from the Shakespearean text. These are described as follows:

- *presentation* (in which the film tries to stay as close to the verbal text as possible)
- *interpretation* (in which the film respects the text but also insists on its own artistic integrity)
- *adaptation* (in which the film uses the text as the starting point for something quite different) (1991: 7–16).

Describing Shakespeare films up until the 1970s (his piece was first published in 1976), Jorgens' categories alert us to some general differences between productions, yet are much too broad to usefully register the diverse modes of appropriative practices in contemporary Shakespeare films. Seven years after Jorgens' taxonomic assertions first came into print, Dudley Andrew proposed three more sub-terms, including 'borrowing' (which 'makes no claims to fidelity'), 'intersecting' (which 'attempts to recreate the distinctions of the original text') and 'transforming' (which 'reproduces the essential text') (1984: 33–4). Recent scholarship has clarified the complexity of adaptation and the need for a scrutinising analysis of numerous factors when contemplating this area of study. For example, James Naremore has suggested that 'the study of adaptation needs to be joined with the study of recycling, remaking, and every other form of retelling in the age of mechanical reproduction and electronic communication' (2000: 15). Naremore's observation of a relationship between textual retelling and mechanical reproduction signals a correlation between the mass production of original works of art (rendering Vincent van Gogh's art works as postcards, for example) and the logic of adaptation, which coheres with the reproduction of original literary works copious amounts of times in diverse ways.

Additional scholarship notes textual transposition for screen as necessarily cutting, replacing, updating or interpolating the text to suit the grammar and vocabulary of visual media (see Cartmell 1999). Others consider notions of intertextuality, nostalgia, remaking, cultural and political frameworks, audience response or 'fandom', and the problematic issue of originality, all of which circumnavigate and infiltrate the term 'adaptation' (see Jenkins 1992 and Verevis 2005). In general, the author emerges in these readings as less an originating agent than a figure bound by the ramifications of what Harold Bloom (1973) called 'the anxiety of influence', always indebted to previous literature whether conscious of it or not. The 'plurality of meaning' that is foregrounded by adaptation denies the author as a single source of meaning, serving instead to suture the multiple points of origin in a text's conception (Cartmell 1999: 28). Influence, according to Bloom's reading, posits that 'there are no texts but only relationships between texts' (1975: 3). The relationship between text and screen is thus argued to facilitate an understanding of the text as 'a multi-dimensional space in which a variety of writings, none of them original, blend and clash', or 'a tissue of quotations drawn from innumerable centres of culture' (Barthes 1995: 126). Yet this relationship is also fraught with cultural tensions, resulting in a hierarchy of a sacrosanct 'original' text and a filmic derivative that is disavowed as a 'new' entity in its own right.

A study of adaptation also involves an examination of the circumstances of production. For example, the production of adaptations at a particular historical juncture may suggest much about the cultural and political climate of their social environment. Courtney Lehmann (2005) recently argued for the proliferation of *King Lear* films – such as *The King Is Alive*, which is addressed in this chapter, Uli Edel's 2002 TV-film *King of Texas* and Don Boyd's *My Kingdom* (2001) – and the play's notions of overwrought kingship, senility and divinely-constituted social authority depicted in these films as symptomatic of the 'senile capitalism' of the George W. Bush administration. Ginette Vincendeau observes the emergence of 'heritage cinema' during the 1980s – a term that denotes 'costume films made in the past twenty years or so, usually based on "popular classics" (Forster, Austen, Shakespeare, Balzac, Dumas, Hugo, Zola)' – as indicative of a nostalgic turn in popular culture that simultaneously legitimated 'challenge[s] to mainstream representations of gender and sexuality', and facilitated feminist revisionist adaptation, such as Emma Thompson's of Jane Austen's *Sense and Sensibility* (1995) 'which reads Austen's novel as a female empowerment text' (2001: xx). James Tweedie reads *Prospero's Books* as a 'meditation on the literary artefact and neo-baroque aesthetics in opposition to the discourse of heritage circulating in Thatcherite Britain' (2000: 104). *The King Is Alive*, moreover, can be argued as responding to its historical moment in terms of cinema's evolution and – says Dogme 95 – its decline at the end of its first century.

A second point of critical enquiry in the study of adaptation is textual transposition. It is important to note that the transposition from text to screen is not a one-way street. Despite Peter Greenaway's proclamation that *Prospero's Books* 'is not a straight attempt to reproduce a familiar text' (quoted in Vincendeau 2001: xxiii), the film's notable obsession with the materiality of the text, alongside the three books that Greenaway published to accompany the film's release (which provided information on the film's conceptual and production origins, as well as a novel, *Prospero's Creatures*, and the script) denote an obvious literary priority at the heart of Greenaway's authorial intention. Similarly, it is common practice to publish a film's screenplay after its release whether the book is derived from a textual source or not, and highly popular productions (such as *The Lord of the Rings* (2001, 2002, 2003) and *The Matrix* (1999, 2003, 2003) trilogies) are often followed by texts which provide detail on elements of the film's production. Although such textual affiliations do not 'transpose' or adapt the film's narrative for a literary work, it is nonetheless crucial to examine the governing factors of the production of a film's textual counterparts. One argument is that the literary element legitimates or 'authorises' a film as a work of high cultural value. The perpetuating ideology of cinema as a low-class apparatus for the masses that, as early as 1899, was raised a rung on the cultural ladder by representations of Shakespeare's plays, has remained remarkably unchanged. Fredric Jameson's description of 'the failure of the new, the imprisonment in the past' as a characteristic of postmodernity belies a larger cultural denouncement of contemporary cinematic reproduction as inferior and, worse, a dominant reason why 'stylistic innovation is no longer possible' (1988: 18). In this reading, literary invocation, instead of cinematic innovation, sums up film's continuing inferiority as an artistic medium.

On the other hand, however, the increasing production of books to accompany a film's release suggests an emergent 'cine-literate' spectatorship, or audiences who are acutely adept at 'reading' films and wish to engage with circumstantial or aesthetic aspects of a film's production, as indicated by DVD 'extras' that increasingly provide viewers with glimpses of deleted scenes and outtakes, crew and cast commentaries, interviews and 'behind the scenes' documentaries. This amount of 'extratextual referentiality'[2] surrounding contemporary film production arguably unmoors the term 'adaptation' from its original 'text-to-screen' conceptual trajectory, offering instead the possibility of a more critical understanding of film's ontology, as well as that of the text. As an example, the interpretive journey that is pursued when spectating a film is comparable to the act of reading. Wolfgang Iser describes the novel as 'a system of perspectives designed to transmit the individuality of the author's vision', and outlines four primary perspectives: 'the narrator, the characters, the plot, and the fictitious reader', each of which come together at a 'meeting point', which is 'the meaning of the text' (1978: 35). Similarly, four perspectives occupy film: the narrator/main character, the director, the characters and the spectator. A film is 'read' in terms of the dynamics and grammar of the medium, and, like a novel, may generate additional 'perspectives', such as intertextual references and allusions, plot elements that correspond to a particular genre, aesthetic rudiments, and socio-political or historical contexts that generate meaning in a specific manner. The interaction of and dialogue between the film and literary text is heightened in the event of an adaptation, as it becomes necessary for spectators to contend with the dynamics of two 'textual' mediums.

In the case of Shakespeare, a further medium is added to the mix: theatre. Shakespeare's plays were not written to be read like books, but were composed strictly to be performed on the Renaissance stage. Though the plays are largely devoid of specific stage directions, they consistently draw attention to their intended theatrical environment, as in *Henry V*:

> But pardon, and gentles all,
> The flat unraised spirits that have dared
> On this unworthy scaffold to bring forth
> So great an object. Can this cock-pit hold
> The vasty fields of France? Or may we cram
> Within this wooden O the very casques
> That did affright the air at Agincourt?
> ...
> And let us, ciphers to this great account,
> On your imaginary forces work.
> Suppose within the girdle of these walls
> Are now confined two mighty monarchies,
> Whose high upreared and abutting fronts
> The perilous narrow ocean parts asunder.

Piece out our imperfections with your thoughts:
Into a thousand parts divide on man,
And make imaginary puissance.
Think, when we talk of horses, that you see them
Printing their proud hoofs i'th' receiving earth;
For 'tis your thoughts that now must deck our kings... (1.1.8–28)

The Chorus at the beginning of *Henry V* asks the play's audiences to visualise what the theatre cannot convey, or to imagine 'the vasty fields of France' crammed within the 'wooden O' of London's round Rose theatre. That Shakespeare calls upon his spectators to perform such imaginative acts – with an acknowledgement of the restrictions of the 'unworthy scaffold' of the theatre in representing French vistas and the exciting scenes of Agincourt – suggests a particularly 'cinematic' longing embedded within the fabric of his texts. While many scholars, critics and directors have debated the cinematic rubric of Shakespeare's plays, gestures towards 'rare visions' and depictions of visual projections are common throughout the body of his work, and should be taken into consideration when the subject of film adaptation is encountered.

A final area of consideration pertinent to this study is the notion of 'bad quartos', or rewritten publications of Shakespeare's plays which are considered erroneous. Shakespeare's original manuscripts are now lost, though these were used to print 'true, originall copies' of his plays as early as 1594 as small pamphlets (quartos) before the more expensive folio volumes of his works began to be printed in 1623. Bearing in mind that only half the plays were printed during his lifetime, it is assumed that Shakespeare rarely (if ever) participated in the editing or publication of his works, resulting in 'bad quartos' which re-tell the original play from memory, favour a subordinate character's point of view, and omit characters, lines and even scenes from the original play. Compositors at printing houses during the early modern period often misread lines and words, resulting in confused metaphors and ineffective language – for instance, Hamlet's famous line, 'to be or not to be, that is the question' in the second quarto of 1605 is 'to be or not to be, ay there's the point' in the first quarto of 1603. The folio editions gradually restored much of Shakespeare's original work. The cheaper quarto rewritings, however, filtered errors into the plays that continue into today's versions. Although Shakespeare's 'bad quartos' are largely due to

early modern methods of publishing, the notion of corruption, collaboration and re-casting inherent in this mode of adaptation continues to inform
and interest contemporary adaptations, and is a useful point of contrast in
examining filmic appropriation.

Creating the illustrated text

> I don't think we've seen any cinema yet.
> I think we've seen 100 years of illustrated text.
> – Peter Greenaway (quoted in Abbot 1997)

Peter Greenaway's self-proclaimed 'adaptation of William Shakespeare's
The Tempest, *Prospero's Books*, is actually a filmic study of the process
of creating a new cinematic work from a number of colliding mediums
and texts. A trained mural painter with an English literary education and a
serious interest in Renaissance art, Greenaway turned to film in the 1960s
after working as a film editor at the Central Office of Information (COI) in
London. As recently as 1994, however, he remarked: 'I still consider myself
a painter, but one who happens to be working in cinema' (quoted in Cody
1994). Greenaway's interest in painting, in particular the corporeality
and textuality inherent in early modern art,[3] pervades his body of work
to the extent that each 'film' experiments in various ways with fusions of
literature, painting and cinema. For example, his 1996 adaptation of Sei
Shonagon's thousand-year-old novel, *The Pillow Book*, visits the notion of
Japanese painting, or calligraphy, as applied to the naked human body.
'Here', as Greenaway puts it, 'absolutely conjoined, is the idea of image
and text, in bed, magnificently copulating together' (quoted in Hawthorne
1997). Greenaway's interest is clearly not in depicting the events of
Shonagon's novel, but in conceptualising its investments in 'sex and text'
(ibid.). Similarly, *Prospero's Books* does not seek to remain faithful to
Shakespeare's play, but departs from its rich weave of extratextual connections and reflexive gestures towards the authorial art, magic and the
theatre to create a mural in motion, or an illustrated text that celebrates
the 'copulation' of a variety of mediums.

   Prospero's Books is discussed here in three important contexts:
Greenaway's exploration of adaptation as a palimpsest or conflation of
textual and extratextual sources, thereby subverting the exclusive sanc-

tity of the 'original' and alerting us to writing as a collaborative art; the film's presentation of adaptation as a 'birthing' process, breathing movement (and thus, life) into the text to create a new, 'original' text; and Greenaway's consideration of an 'original' text as an irrevocably hybrid formation. The common denominator of these three areas of enquiry is, as Lia M. Hotchkiss observes, 'the production of the text' (2002: 96), or the reproduction of the text as a living entity.

Prospero's Books imagines *The Tempest* as a series of textual networks and transmissions. Pivoting on the lines, 'Knowing I loved my books, he furnished me/From mine own library with volumes that/I prized above my dukedom' (1.2.167–9), the film imagines Gonzalo's merciful donation of Prospero's much-loved books to suggest Prospero's powers of witchcraft and wizardry as part of a 'generative bibliographic exchange' (Murphy 2000: 14). Although the play does not elaborate on Prospero's library, a comment by Caliban in Act Three underscores the magical potency of these books, containing within their leaves the source of Prospero's power: 'Remember/First to possess his books, for without them/He's but a sot as I am, nor hath not/One spirit to command' (3.2.86–9). In departure from Caliban's reasoning, the film gestures towards a triangular configuration of authorial creation: Prospero, as life-giving author, Greenaway's 'technological wizardry' and Shakespeare's textual craft (Rothwell 2004: 199). The film's juxtaposition of three authorial sources posits originality as a reframing of existing material, and authorship as involving the creation of new texts using old ones, as opposed to a 'conjuring' act as figured in Méliès' film. It would be easy to suggest Greenaway's portrait of originality and authorship as mere intertextuality or citation, yet thorough examination of this production demonstrates how Greenaway collates and crashes mediums, authors, technology and artistic influences to present 'originality' as multivalent and polyphonic.

Prospero's Books opens with one of the most elaborate and artistically-rendered sequences in the history of Shakespeare on film. Following extreme close-ups of drops of water accompanied by loud dripping sounds the film introduces 'The Book of Water', in which 'watery elements are often animated' as images in motion, or small films, portraying 'rippling waves and slanting storms' (Greenaway 1991: 17). Scenes of writing are inserted and superimposed upon a subsequent scene in which Prospero (Sir John Gielgud) stands naked in an indoor swimming pool with a small model-sized ship, reading the opening lines of the play aloud. The *mise-en-scène* is composed of a series of triadic superimpositions, compressing images of 'The Book of Water' upon shots of Prospero-as-performer in the swimming pool with additional shots of Prospero-as-author, robed in his library and scribing Shakespeare's play. The drops of water – which sound

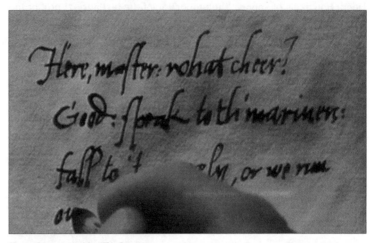

Fig. 3: Prospero writing *The Tempest*

Fig. 4: Superimposing the author and the text

like heartbeats – are soon replaced with rhythmic blasts of fire, and the credit sequence begins at the site of Prospero's swimming pool. A host of naked men and women and, oddly enough, llamas emerge from the pillars, as though brought to life by Prospero's writings. Throughout the credit sequences the camera tracks slowly past the pillars and naked figures as Prospero walks – surrounded by four dancing figures – towards his library. As the pulsing blasts of fire cease, the sound of a hammer hitting an anvil is heard, again in a heartbeat rhythm. The camera tracks for four minutes, showing – symbolically behind the credits – a book being passed along semi-naked figures who dance mechanically, suggesting them as robotic constructs of Prospero's authorial power. Michael Nyman's minimalist score comes to an end, allowing only the sounds of the anvil, scream and owls to be heard beneath the bombast of a storm.

This opening sequence concretises many of Greenaway's conceptual approaches explored throughout his other works. In particular, his use of what might be described as a 'mural aesthetic', consistently tracking from left to right past scenes that depict the text as a moving mural, shows the illustrated text as one that is constantly in motion, not only in terms of its filmic portraits but also in its motion between historical eras, translators, adaptors, directors and performers. In addition, the text here is a signifier of different kinds of movement and expression; the text is never fixed or closed, but constantly available for potential meanings and adaptations to come forth from it. French literary theorist Jacques Derrida makes a similar comment in *Writing and Difference*:

> the book is original ... everything *belongs to the book* before being and in order to come into the world; that any thing can be born only by *approaching* the book, can die only by failing *in sight of* the book; and that always the impassible short of the book is *first*. (1978: 77)

Whereas the book is usually revered as the material site of an 'original' text, Greenaway sees the book as the site of potential meanings, or, as Derrida remarks, a 'differential network, a fabric of traces, referring endlessly to something other than itself' (1979: 84). The abundance of characters, allusions, sounds and movements in this opening sequence is in keeping with the film's subsequent layers of visual meanings and puns. Yet the sheer density of the *mise-en-scène* runs the risk of drowning Greenaway's film text under the weight of indexical traces (see also Tweedie 2000: 114). Indeed, the film's narrative, though moving steadily towards the outcome detailed in Shakespeare's play, is often overburdened by Greenaway's 'mural aesthetic' – or the number of frames, movements, images and characters – which demands careful attention if any amount of allusions are to be noted and appreciated. Yet the conceptual currency of the production is evident in terms of both the specificity of detail and obvious links between textuality and creation. As the opening sequence suggests – confirmed by a later shot of Prospero's wife whilst pregnant with Miranda peeling back the skin of her abdomen to reveal her internal organs and growing foetus – Shakespeare's text is regarded as the site of creation, a kind of authorial 'womb' from which endless textual 'offspring' are born.

Of course, Prospero's powers are not entirely keeping with the laws of nature. The books are configured as somewhat human entities, replete with lungs and physical form that must be deprived of oxygen if they are to be terminated. Yet Prospero's magic is not maternal, nor strictly paternal, as suggested by the sounds of the hammer and anvil during the credit sequence, which indicate the almost medieval, industrial creation of Prospero's subjects. Other images of pregnancy and birth throughout the film are shown in complete subversion to nature. Sycorax is shown as a bald-headed male whilst giving birth to Caliban. Sounds of pigs and other animals grunting accompany the short scene, whilst Prospero's voice-over suggests the unnatural circumstances of Caliban's birth: 'a freckled whelp hag-born – not honour'd with/A human shape' (1.2.285–6). The same scene depicts the tree in which Sycorax 'did confine [Caliban],/By help of her more potent ministers/And in her most unmitigable rage,/Into a cloven pine' (1.2.276–79) for twelve years. As Prospero threatens Ariel with a similar imprisonment, a series of shots show Ariel (enacting Caliban) screaming as the tree drags him into its 'knotty entrails' (1.2.297), then spewing blood and insects, and crying as the bark of the tree overtakes his skin. What is suggested in both sequences is the subversion of nature. Birth is shown in its most grotesque form to be animalistic and attributed to witches, whilst Caliban's second 'birth' is an unnatural entombing within a tree from which Prospero frees him.

In short, Prospero's originating, authorial powers are subversive *derivatives* of nature. Prospero employs various forms of water in place of amniotic fluid, for instance, as a gestational substance for his textual creations. The paradox inherent in Prospero's power originating from nature suggests that the idea of the original in the film is in keeping with the impossibility of an 'original', as all meanings (and texts) derive from a primary point of origin that cannot be located. The notion of an adaptation presupposes the existence of an 'original' text, yet the original is never a 'pure' text, nor is it unaffected by others. The original is both a derivative and distorted by its own derivatives, suggesting adaptations as both a backward *and* forward textual motion.

Driving the film's interest in the impossibility of originality is the notion of adaptation as a hybrid practice. Whereas adaptation theorists tend to camp within the disparate debates of fidelity and infidelity, Greenaway opts for a slant on what Robert Stam defines as 'intertextual dialogism' (2000: 64). Insisting upon the creation of a dialogue between texts, Stam's term additionally suggests 'the infinite and open-ended possibilities generated by all the discursive practices of a culture, the entire matrix of communicative utterances within which the artistic text is situated' (ibid.). The 'dialogue' of Greenaway's film, however, is between so many modes, texts, historical locations and figures that there is no clear depiction of who started the conversation, nor of what is being said. In reflection of this, one character speaks for another on many occasions throughout the film. A scene showing Antonio and Sebastian in 'conversation' shows subtitles of Shakespeare's text (and uttered by Prospero) whilst the characters themselves remain close-mouthed. Processes of birth, dialogue and hybridisation therefore figure in the film to represent adaptation as an endless 'mural' of narratives, aesthetics and interpretive possibilities that are constantly in movement and conflict.

Caliban serves to embody this idea of adaptation. Identified in Shakespeare's play as a being of many potential forms, Caliban is recounted by Prospero as being born without a human shape, and is later suggested by Gonzalo as in possession of a 'monstrous shape' (3.3.31). This is in concert with Trinculo's comment when he stumbles upon Caliban: 'What have we here? a man or a fish? dead or alive?' (2.2.23–4). Caliban's true shape is never identified in the play, but rather is observed and described by other characters, including Trinculo's wry comment that, back in England, 'there would this monster make a man' for 'any strange beast there makes a man' (2.2.29). As other critics have noted, Caliban serves in Greenaway's film to embody the attributes and 'shape' of a derivative text (see Tweedie 2000: 119). Caliban here, played by Michael Clark, no more resembles a fish or monster than does Prospero. Bald-headed and naked (except for body markings), Caliban appears as 'monstrous' only in deed, not form. Likewise, adaptations are often regarded as 'monstrous', bastardised and generally vulgar imitations of an original that smear its very existence by coming into being. Stam comments:

> The language of criticism dealing with [film adaptation] has often been profoundly moralistic, awash in terms such as *infidelity*, *betrayal*, *deformation*, *violation*, *vulgarisation*, and *desecration*, each accusation carrying its specific charge of outraged negativity. (2000: 54)

Caliban not only embodies the adaptation's sense of 'vulgarisation' but also enacts its functions of 'violation' and 'desecration' by urinating and defecating on the books and by slashing their pages. This is because he identifies them as the source of Prospero's power and authority. As Derrida argued, the book is the source of power and authority; the cultural veneration surrounding it defines it as an 'original', as a source. For Caliban, the threat of the books lies precisely in their containment of 'originality'. Likewise, in the age of mechanical reproduction, as stated earlier, the threat of originality is contained by apparatuses such as those presented in Greenaway's film. Just as Prospero is able to magically conjure countless spirits and textual characters into being – or, conversely, to drown them – so too is cinema able 'magically' to reproduce, copy and illustrate the text according to an endless list of possible illustrations and interpretations. It is possibly this last context – interpretation – that underlines the real threat of adaptation. What if a text is illustrated according to meanings not found in the original? What if new meanings are created in contradiction to those of the original? Will new interpretations and meanings replace the original? Will these interpretations effectively, as Caliban wishes, kill the author of the original? How do we reconcile or differentiate between the original and its multiple adaptations?

For Greenaway, neither reconciliation nor differentiation is possible. The original already contains all the possibilities that come forth from it that in turn construct the original as a cultural, intertextual event. The film's frame-within-frames and superimposed shots register the presence of existing adaptations within the frames of subsequent adaptations. This is shown to be neither entirely reflexive nor entirely compromising to an adaptation's 'originality', but instead is an integral part of the creative process. Shakespeare's text is additionally observed here as part of a collaborative exchange instead of an isolated authorial creation. By showing the book being passed along throughout the credit sequence, Greenaway signals 'his awareness of his own involvement in the ongoing process of textual transmission', demonstrating his appropriational 'text' as part of an ongoing series of readings, translations and re-writings (Buchanan 2005: 174). The book in which Prospero is writing, for example, is 'The Book of Thirty-Six Plays', described as 'a thick, printed volume of plays dated 1623' with the first 19 pages left blank for the inclusion of the first (and 37th) play: that which Prospero is writing (Greenaway 1991: 34). But on the front of the book the author's initials, W. S., are engraved in gold – an obvious reference to William Shakespeare. The film's aesthetic and narrative structure is organised according to this logic of books as frames-within-frames, or books-within-books. Consequently, adaptation is presented as not strictly collaborative, but as a palimpsestuous re-making of meaning within the meshes of authored texts. 'Originality' is thus a dialectical by-product or 'offspring' of texts; it never involves a blank page.

Greenaway's study of adaptation in *Prospero's Books* culminates in a final, hotly-discussed shot of Ariel leaping towards the spectator out of frame. This shot is regarded by Andrew Murphy as suggesting that at this point 'the film, far from breaking out of the cinematic frame, in fact collapses in on itself, sucked back into the vanishing point of the author and his singular, isolated text' (2000: 18). Alternatively, James Tweedie suggests Ariel's final ascent 'into a site that is neither a book page nor a cinematic space but something in between' (2000: 122). The importance of the frame at this point is, as these critics observe, absolutely crucial, and is preceded by Prospero's 'drowning' of his books as captured by a series of frames showing once more the pages and contents of the books in an insert as they drift under water. A close-up of Gielgud reciting the epilogue moves backwards, figuring the image as a floating frame in a black background. Upon Gielgud's utterance of the closing line, 'upon your indulgence set me free' (Epilogue, 20), the close-up forms a background against another close-up of a splash of water (reprising the water drops at the beginning), from which Ariel emerges and runs past the other applauding characters towards the camera frame, which is pulling backwards towards the spectator. After a number of water drops and flame blasts, a younger Ariel appears and runs towards us, captured in slow motion as his background changes to parchment – Orpheus' Atlas of Hades – and leaps up and 'over' the frame. To former analyses of this scene can be added the view that Greenaway asserts the film as a 'frame' within the series of adaptations that derive from the 'original'.

The two spaces of the diegesis that become apparent here – the space of the film and that of the film's spectator – are crossed over by Ariel, as if passing into the frame of a subsequent adaptation of Shakespeare's play that will, no doubt, be aware of and possibly influenced by Greenaway's film. Ariel operates here as the trace of Greenaway's production, transcending the film's frame as the embodiment of Walter Benjamin's (1969) conception of the 'aura' of the original. But instead of being pilfered or 'vulgarised' by subsequent productions, Ariel-as-aura announces the film's own originality as a 'new' work, despite its derivative nature, and in turn offers himself freely to other appropriations of the play as an intertextual presence. In addition, the integrity or 'frame' of the original is broken and transcended, leaving us with a view of a book that, again by its mythical association (of Orpheus leaving the Underworld under strict instruction not to look back upon Eurydice), infers that adaptation involves the murky exploration of 'dead' texts to which one often should not look back.

The film's effectiveness no doubt lies in its powerful, wide-ranging consideration of textuality and adaptation. But this is at the risk of leaving the viewer emotionally cold and in the dark as to what Shakespeare's play is actually about. Moreover, adaptation is explored here as an almost chaotic series of textual links and possibilities, yet the collision and conflation of art forms is never entirely convincing in Greenaway's creation of a 'new' form of 'illustrated text'. On the other hand, however, Greenaway succeeds in radically reinvigorating Shakespeare's play and, at the very least, prompts us to regard Shakespeare films not as faithful representations that replace (or save us from reading) the original play, but as composites, or hybrids, of aesthetic, social, interpretive, historical and technological formats and perspectives.

Will the real author please stand up?

> 'This play ... what's it all about?'
> – Ray, *The King Is Alive*

The underlining notion of textual re-production and re-birth in *Prospero's Books* continues in Kristian Levring's *The King Is Alive* in the context of authorship. Here Shakespeare's *King Lear* is performed by a group of stranded tourists in the middle of the Namibian desert while they wait to be rescued, taking refuge in abandoned mining sheds. In accordance with the play's slightly troubled textual history – currently existing as a conflated version of two differing quartos published in 1608 (titled *The History of King Lear*) and 1623 (titled *The Tragedy of King Lear*) – the film depicts the re-writing of *King Lear* from the memory of one of the tourists, who is a former stage actor. Evocative of the 'bad quarto' debacle, the play is recounted intact for the most part, but is simultaneously dissected to reveal the relationship(s) between the 'original' and its adaptations. Moreover, the performance of the play affects the reality of the tourists until each of them face the same fate as their characters, whilst the play's 'author', Henry (David Bradley), assumes Lear's woeful fate as a father-figure who loses his beloved Cordelia and becomes truly lost not in the desert, but within the pages of Shakespeare's text. The 'king' in this production is suggested as the author, who becomes and remains 'alive' whilst the characters of the play and film die off. But who, the film asks, is the 'real' author? Henry, Levring or Shakespeare?

In his essay 'The Death of the Author' French literary critic Roland Barthes argued that the original authorial intentions behind a text's production are irrelevant to a reader's interpretation of the text. In closing his essay, Barthes puts his point succinctly: 'the birth of the reader must be at the cost of the death of the Author' (1995: 130). Yet the presence of the author is not restricted to his or her textual intentions. Adaptations play a part in circulating the text amongst various cultures and historical contexts, often imposing upon the author cultural authority that is almost impossible to disregard when encountering a text. This is in part what Michel Foucault was referring to in his description of the 'author-function'. Reminding us that the author is a conceptual identity that changes over time, Foucault argues that the author-function defines the way in which the author does not determine the text's meanings, but acts as a unifying force by which the text's contextual interpretations and cultural appropriations are bonded and understood. In adaptation studies, the importance of the author is often overlooked in the pursuit of textual strategies and categories that define the process by which a text is visualised on-screen. However, both an original text and its subsequent adaptations or translations are produced, and unified, by an author or authors. As a result, the notion of authorship as a single unit becomes increasingly problematic and hard to define.

These notions of authorship and adaptation are consonant with the central concerns of Dogme 95, the manifesto-movement framing *The King Is Alive*.[4] Dogme 95 was established by Danish filmmakers Lars von Trier, Thomas Vinterberg, Søren Kragh-Jacobsen and Kristian Levring at the international symposium in Paris, 'Le cinéma vers son deuxième siècle', on the centennial anniversary of the Lumière brothers' primary cinema screening in Paris. From its outset, Dogme was intended to overturn the apparent state of decay in mainstream cinema by re-exploring the minimalistic production techniques of the Lumières to create original, 'new' productions. The movement claimed that 'the old film is dead', announcing that 'we believe in the new' (see von Trier & Vinterberg 2000: 6–7). Its founders established a list of ten rules known as 'The Vow of Chastity' to which filmmakers had to subscribe if they wanted their film to be known as a 'Dogme' film. In return, a certificate of 'authenticity' was issued that could be shown at the beginning of the film. In accordance with the Vow, Levring's film is shot on location in Namibia using digital video without filters, artificial light or non-diegetic music. In particular, the manifesto states that the director of a Dogme film must not be credited, perhaps in keeping with the tradition of early films that, as Emmanuelle Toulet points out, 'announced the name of the film and the production house [yet] the names of the director, actors and technicians would long remain anonymous' (1995: 51). Levring's name *does* appear in the film alongside the names of the actors, and not in conjunction with the caption 'directed by', suggesting that Levring is another member of the group of tourists, part of the film's audience. Thus, the film's author is not immediately apparent.

This is because several authors appear in the film. Henry's inspiration for re-writing *King Lear* comes during a moment of reflection upon the group's first alcohol-drenched night in the middle of the desert. Watching the rest of the group deal with their hangovers and desperate situation, Henry says aloud 'is man no more than this?', a line from Shakespeare's play uttered by Lear in the context of his enforced exile. The next scene shows Henry writing the different parts of the play by hand on scrolls in one of the sheds. Not all of the parts are included, however. In Levring's words, 'the play [Henry] stages is the *King Lear* of his memory, modified to fit with the people he has at his disposal. In that way he makes it a Dogme *King Lear*' (Rundle 1999). Levring's interpretation of Henry's authorship pitches the performance as less a rewriting than a recollection of Shakespeare's play that conveniently serves the political agenda of the film's manifesto movement. Of course, Levring here is drawing attention to Henry's pared-down rendition of the play, writing on old scrolls patched together with sticking plasters, using rusting gas barrels as props and employing the most unlikely of casts – all of which are meant to correspond with Dogme's back-to-basics approach to filmmaking. In theory, Dogme's aim to 'return to the innocence and simplicity' of the Lumière brothers involves a disa-vowal of the authority of the author, privileging the film text as the vehicle of originality. But, as the film's characters indicate, neither the text nor its author exerts control over their interpretations of or responses to the play.

These interpretations and responses overlap and depart from Shakes-peare's play in many ways. Liz (Janet McTeer) as both Goneril and Regan brings new meaning to the line 'I must change arms at home, and give the distaff/Into my husband's hands' (4.2.17–18). At this point in the film her resentment of Ray (Bruce Davison), her husband, has reached its peak, as she insists upon repeating the line over and over and concluding the speech by kissing Moses (as Edmund, played by Vusi Kunene) in front of Ray. Having previously (and unsuccessfully) tried to force Moses to have sex with her, Liz now uses her role to interpret Goneril's line – which means that she must become the masculine figure at home whilst her husband adopts a feminine role – to suggest her decision to cuckold Ray. This decision has echoes of Goneril's meaning running through it. The tension between Ray and Liz likewise correlates with the action of the play. Ray's comment on Regan and Goneril's ill-treatment of their father is met by Liz's bitter retort, 'At least he had a daughter'. The suggestion is that their mari-tal problems are caused by their childlessness. Liz's attempted rape of Moses indicates a desperate attempt to get pregnant; Goneril's comment 'My fool usurps my body' (4.2.28) and her efforts throughout the play to oust Lear are transferred during the desert performance to the issues of Liz's childlessness and unresolved marital conflict.

Each of the film's characters enliven and re-interpret the play from their own perspectives, suggesting the prioritisation of the reader – or performer – over both the text and author. Says Barthes, 'the reader is the space on which all the quotations that make up a writing are inscribed without any of them being lost; a text's unity lies not in its origin but in its destination' (1995: 126). Barthes' concept of 'destination' is implied as being the reader, who is responsible therefore for textual unity. Yet this is not exactly accurate either. The film conveys overlaps between the characters' responses to and interpretations of the play and those that exist within the play already. As Ray's comment indicates ('This play … I mean, what's it all about?'), not all the performers are familiar with the work, and Shakespeare is never mentioned. Yet still they find meanings within it that pertain to their individual contexts which do not depart completely from the 'destination' of the original text. This is most likely because, of course, the whole situation is contrived by the film's author, Kristian Levring. While the notion of textual unity is an ideal, it is insufficient to relegate it to one space entirely. As the film observes, we can never be entirely sure of the proper definitions of 'reader', 'text', 'original' or 'author'. The readers within the film are bound by an already prescribed narrative 'destination'; Levring is bound by Dogme's Vow and manifesto; and we, the film's readers, do not have 'all the quotations'. Our ability to create textual unity, or indeed to reconcile between original, adaptation and their intertextual connections is limited because, like Henry's scrolls pieced together with plasters and written as fragments of memory, we always contend with the 'original' text in fragmentation and distortion.

In sum, a consideration of the role of the author is vital when examining adaptations. Levring's film ultimately aspires to be collaborative – recalling early-modern writing circumstances – but never manages to completely throw off the author 'problem'. Instead, the author is multiplied. Dogme's manifesto – written by Levring and three others – appears as a dominating force through the production, guiding both Levring's interpretation of the play and his methods of narrating it. The idea of a 'Dogme *King Lear*' may seem ironic, but it is suggestive of a fourth 'authorial' presence in the film. Yet the Dogme manifesto is a re-iteration of previous manifestos (such as the manifesto of New German Cinema in 1962), which looks to cinema's forefathers as the benchmark of cinematic purity. Who, then, can be identified as the author(s) of Dogme's manifesto – Levring *et al.*, the authors of the manifesto of New German Cinema, or the Lumières? In this light, who exactly is the author of this 'Dogme *King Lear*'?

What each of these problems and issues in the film indicates is that 'the death of the author' happens not entirely in the event of the birth of the reader, but in the event of the creation of an 'author-as-reader'. The textual network identified by both Foucault and Barthes indicates the circulation of texts to the extent that boundaries are impossible to draw between a text and its 'original' meaning. What an adaptation can alert us to, however, is a similar blurring of boundaries between an author and an adaptor. In both cases, the destination is never strictly forward: the text is always looking back.

Conclusions

Shakespeare-as-author has come to signify the process of adaptation and exchange much more than he operates as a single, unifying force of textual meaning. Shakespeare's apparent 'infinite adaptability' has been noted throughout 'a variety of cultures and languages', and has long been attributed to the inherent 'universality' of the plays (Billington 1996: 15). While the plays do indeed grapple with many 'universal' themes such as death, love, revenge, murder and duplicity, it is important to remember that they are also rooted in their particular historical and social context – Shakespeare's language being a major part of this context. The infinite adaptability of the plays might therefore be perceived as deriving from something more than Shakespeare, the author. Consider Dudley Andrew's comment in this regard:

> every representational film adapts a prior conception. Indeed, the very term *representation* suggests the existence of a model. Adaptation delimits representation by insisting on the cultural status of the model, on its existence in the mode of the text or the already textualised. (1984: 29)

Put briefly, Shakespeare is continually textualised; adaptations do not merely return to the original play, but negotiate 'prior conceptions' of the play across various historical periods and media. That is not to say that every version of *Twelfth Night* is responding to every previous version of the play; but it is important to remember that 'the existence of a model' is an important element in adaptation, which forces us to approach with care notions of 'originality', authorship and adaptation.

The film examples examined in this chapter have considered adaptation as both a collaborative and hybrid exercise, often involving the superimposition of a number of texts and subsequently throwing notions of fidelity and textual 'essence' into question. Adaptation theory invariably visits the idea of textual transposition, but as both films demonstrate, the film medium offers a specific kind of textuality that does not always resonate entirely with the literary text. Added to this are a number of new media formats and technologies which allow us to consider different kinds of 'texts', such as the hypertext (an interactive text), metatext (a text about textuality) and paratext (an external textual material surrounding a text, such as commentaries, DVD features, sequels and so forth), each of which underline the idea of 'textuality' in general as a dialogue between textual sources that is shaped by the properties or 'grammar' of particular media, be they literary, filmic, digital or electronic (see Landow 1991; Genette 1997; Manovich 2002). Each of these forms necessarily prompts a reconsideration of methods of 'reading' the text according to the properties of its medium, as we shall see in the following chapter.

Finally, it is important to examine the ways in which adaptations circulate social discourses and ideologies, which requires us not only to negotiate dialogues between texts but also to analyse the ideological positions that are generated by adaptations (see Stam 2005: 45–6). In short, the process of adapting Shakespeare is never a simple transposition or translation from text to screen; rather, this process responds to the dictates of particular cultural values, social ideologies, technological developments, industrial demands and aesthetic properties, all of which ultimately must inform our reading of the Shakespearean film text as less a straightforward 'original' or 'derivative', but as a cultural event.

3   FILM STYLE

The film text necessarily has a form. Structured according to a system of principles that generates the narration of the film text to an audience, a film's formal system also works alongside a set of stylistic elements, such as *mise-en-scène*, cinematography, editing and sound. As the preceding chapters have indicated, visualising the Shakespearean text involves this combination of aesthetic ingredients. An understanding of film language is vital, therefore, if we are to 'read' a Shakespeare film successfully. Film style involves an exploration of the means by which films generate expressive emotion, reveal narratives, signify meanings, construct related formal patterns and position viewers into particular ideological/moral/emotional relationships with the film text. A full comprehension of film style additionally requires an examination of its determining factors. These include economic restrictions or studio mandates, industrial and technological developments, film trends and conventions, social issues and additional historical contexts that will be considered throughout the following chapter.

Developed at the beginning of the twentieth century as a form of criticism by which to discuss film as an art form, film style divided theorists into two main theoretical 'camps': formalism and realism. In brief, formalists such as Rudolf Arnheim and the Soviet filmmaker Sergei Eisenstein eschewed the idea that film reproduced a photographic copy of reality, arguing that film's formal dimensions offered instead an artistic expression of reality, like a painting (Eisenstein 1949; Arnheim 1957). The opinions put forward by these theorists were later countered by the 'realists', namely André Bazin and Siegfried Kracauer, who argued for film's recording facility as a reproduction of reality (Bazin 1967; Kracauer 1995). The main difference between these two schools of thought is the process of symbolisation or codification announced in formalism, and the sense of 're-present-ation' inherent in realism – literally making the past re-present. Their similarities, however, lie in a notable parallel engagement with film's relationship to reality, and the stylistic techniques that contribute to this relationship. Recent theorists such as Noël Carroll and David Bordwell have usefully observed the diversity of approaches to film style and its historical developments, indicating that the term 'style' has come to refer to many things, such as period style, directorial style (as well as various periods or versions of directorial style), studio style, genre style, school or movement style, classical style and so forth (Carroll 1988: 1–2; Bordwell 1997). Carroll's list of types of style seeks predominantly to contend with the range of factors influencing the production of style. Some of these factors include technological developments, industrial or economic restrictions and directorial style. Each of these factors is concomitant with further determinants, such as the impact of cinematic trends upon directorial style. Other theorists, such as V. F. Perkins, separated style from form, asserting an anti-essentialist approach to film in order to understand the imposition or externality of film style:

> I do not believe that the film (or any other medium) has an *essence* which we can usefully invoke to justify our criteria. We do not deduce the standards relevant to Rembrandt from the essence of paint; nor does the nature of words impose a method of judging ballads and novels. Standards of judgement cannot be appropriate to a medium as such but only to particular ways of exploiting its opportunities. (1993: 59; emphasis added)

In short, style is never fixed – it is constantly in flux. Nonetheless, there are particular formal characteristics of film which, as examined here, prove to be invaluable in appreciating film alongside an exploration of the weight of stylistic factors.

One of these factors is technology. In this regard, it is important to observe briefly the development of film equipment throughout the twentieth century and the many ways in which this enabled various artistic visions to be realised. For instance, it is difficult to appreciate the aesthetic qualities of Franco Zeffirelli's *Romeo and Juliet* (1968) without a knowledge of the 'lighter' 16mm camera that had come into being during the 1960s, permitting filmmakers to remove the camera from the tripod for the first time and benefit from hand-held shots and mobilised cinematography. Also of interest is this film's (over)use of the zoom, which was a new technological advantage and has significant aesthetic characteristics in *Romeo and Juliet*. Michael Almereyda's *Hamlet* parades the wealth of media technologies available to the consumer at the commencement of the twenty-first century, such as digital cameras, Pixelvision, Quicktime and Adobe Photoshop, as well as mobile phones, fax machines, mobile DVD players and in-car entertainment systems. Both of these films show the vital role that technology plays in the imagination and cultural relevance of the Shakespearean text.

A second factor is directorial style. This is perhaps best encountered in comparison with a director's previous or subsequent works. Baz Luhrmann's style, for instance, as displayed in *William Shakespeare's Romeo + Juliet*, *Strictly Ballroom* (1992) and *Moulin Rouge!* (2001), is defined by a consistent pop culture iconography, rapid zooms and montages, manipulated and varied film speeds, a contemporary soundtrack and a recurrent visual gesture to the famous 'Coca-Cola' sign at King's Cross in his home town of Sydney, transposed in these films to 'L'Amour'. Kenneth Branagh frequently uses 360-degree pan shots, long takes and the same cast members in each of his films; Orson Welles' style is defined by precisely orchestrated shots that are heavily symbolic of the narrative as a whole, such as the frequent occurrence of bars and fences in his *The Tragedy of Othello: The Moor of Venice* to represent the 'net' cast by Iago upon his duped subjects.

Welles' film career additionally registers the impact of industrial or economic restrictions on style, and is worth considering briefly here. Although a Hollywood prodigy by his mid-twenties, Welles' artistic genius failed to achieve commercial success and was persistently in conflict with studio control. Welles subsequently struggled throughout his career to realise his aesthetic dreams, often financing his own films by performing in other productions and regularly forced to compromise his film techniques and schedule due to budget restrictions. *Othello*, examined in more detail later in this chapter, reveals only a fraction of its production problems. In reality, this film took over three years to make, and forced Welles on many occasions to improvise entire scenes when funding, costumes or locations fell through. Yet there is evidence of as much directorial virtuosity in his version of *Othello* as there is in his earlier studio-financed début, *Citizen Kane* (1941). Welles proved that his own aesthetic could remain more or less intact with or without studio funding, but at the cost of his career. Note that, in this instance, Welles' historical position was a determinant in his financing problems. During the era of Classical Hollywood, the director was viewed mainly as a mere studio employee, a technician with as much authority as a camera operator. Had Welles lived during a later period, his stylistic prowess might have enjoyed greater industrial liberties and success.

In Shakespearean cinema, film style and the related contexts of this subject are a primary point of intellectual enquiry in understanding the transposition of an early-modern performance text to a twentieth-century medium with its own sharply defined rules and grammar. By visiting film style, we can encounter and perhaps comprehend more fully the 'cinematic logic' of Shakespeare's texts spoken of recently by Kenneth Branagh, or, conversely, perceive the burden of the book on film rhetoric (quoted in Burnett & Wray 2000: 173). Drawing upon Welles' *Othello*, Almereyda's *Hamlet*, Julie Taymor's *Titus* (1999), Luhrmann's *Romeo + Juliet*, Richard Loncraine's *Richard III*, Akira Kurosawa's *Throne of Blood* (1957) and other films, let us now examine four of the major components of film style – *mise-en-scène*, cinematography, editing and sound – in terms of how they shape our analysis of Shakespeare films.

Mise-en-scène

The purpose of *mise-en-scène* is, first and foremost, to create a unity between the film's narrative and its diegesis. That is, everything that occupies the shot, whether used to progress the narrative or not, is a symbolic component of the narrative. The way in which actors are positioned within the frame, the clothes they wear, the type of lighting, the setting and décor, the books or empty whisky bottle on the character's desk – all of these work together to contribute to the narrative and to our interpretation of the character and plot. As a general rule, if a gun is revealed in Act One of a film, it will be used in Act Three (as in Luhrmann's *Romeo + Juliet*). The 'character arc' that the protagonist, or main character, will travel – meaning that he or she will be changed somehow by the end of the film – will often be foreshadowed by the *mise-en-scène* at the film's beginning. Note, for instance, Kenneth Branagh's entrance as the titular character in his *Henry V*, appearing at the threshold of his court. Here a low-angle shot implies his political dominance; the use of a backlight renders him in darkness and Darth Vader-like, conjuring associations with the dark lord of *Star Wars* (1977) in both appearance and, implicitly, his descent from defender of truth to a morally-bankrupt monster. The resplendent setting of Branagh's later film, *Hamlet*, represents the regal façade that is about to crack under the weight of Old Hamlet's colossal ghost. And, as we saw in chapter 1, an actor's performance is often in congruence with the *mise-en-scène*. In Branagh's *Henry V*, for instance, the use of shadows and backlight to suggest the king as a somewhat morally ambiguous character is developed by Branagh's performance as divided between his roles as king and soldier. If there is disunity between the elements of the *mise-en-scène* and the film's narrative, it is usually to portend or infer a disharmony between the film's text and subtext that is later to be revealed.

Welles' *Othello* has been described as an 'authentic flawed masterpiece' (Jorgens 1991: 175). Flawed because of its continuity and sound problems, the film excels in its skilled use of visual imagery. The opening scene lasts just over three minutes and contains 38 shots without dialogue or diegetic music. The action of the scene conveys the bodies of Othello (Welles) and Desdemona (Suzanne Cloutier) being taken for burial; meanwhile the treacherous Iago (Micheál MacLiammóir) is imprisoned in a cage that is slung high above the funeral procession and city crowds. This scene appears before the credits, and is not found in Shakespeare's text. The use of chiaroscuro in the scene establishes the film's noir tone, whilst Welles' use of perspective and deep focus expertly creates a visual texture that insinuates the film's narrative layers.

These narrative layers are created in this scene by visual references to and comparisons between the play's latent dualities. The large Christian cross that is carried in front of Desdemona's body is in contrast to the bars of Iago's cage which, framed tightly against his face and in close-up, appear as upside-down crosses – thus confirming Iago's villainy and paganism in contradiction to the two dead characters, who are implied as morally upright and Christian. The importance of Christian ideologies in this landscape is reiterated by the low-angle shot of two figures crossing themselves, at the same time as the juxtaposed images of the cross

Figs 5 and 6: Courtiers carry Desdemona's (Suzanne Cloutier) body for burial; Iago (Micheàl McLiammóir) peers down from his cage at the crowds below

and bars of Iago's cage anticipate the web of lies which will determine the fate of the two dead figures. Likewise, the connection between the cross and bars that is established here pre-empts Othello's descent from moral virtue to murder, suggesting as a sub-text that the real cage that ensnares Othello is actually an interior character flaw.

Of particular importance in Welles' use of *mise-en-scène* is the conflation of two contrasting film styles (see also Jorgens 1991: 175). The opening sequence is clearly a montage, with each of the shots orchestrating a symbolic relationship between the visual elements that gives rise to a host of meanings and interpretations. Later scenes evidence a more formalistic approach, such as the deep-focus shot of a slapped Desdemona obeying Othello's stern order to 'get you away' (4.1.254), and a slow dissolve from a silhouetted low-angle shot of Iago at the film's beginning as he spies on Desdemona, fading very gradually into a shot of the Venetian waters. In this scene, the superimposition of Iago's image upon the water suggests that what we are seeing is a reflection, and that the 'real' Iago is never seen. He is a fluid entity, able to change shape and form. Like Venice's watery element, Iago is as omnipresent as jealousy. He is at once a demonic character and unmeasured passion in human form.

The two disparate styles that appear in the film are described by Jorgens as 'Othello style' and 'Iago style', the former defined by shots of arches and Venetian architecture, and lattices which seem to imprison characters, either by reflection or long shots which bring characters and their restrictive environment into closer proximity (1991: 177). Conversely, 'Iago style' represents the film's 'dizzying perspectives and camera movements, tortured compositions, grotesque shadows, and insane distortations', for Iago is 'the agent of chaos' (ibid.). To this can be added the view that the two conflicting 'styles' within the film set out to define the dualities within the play – these include black and white, love and envy, (Christian) Venice and (pagan) Cyprus, circles (representing femininity) and bars (masculinity), good and evil and also interiority and externality. But to me it seems that the 'Othello' and 'Iago' styles are apparent not only in the *mise-en-scène*'s treatment of architecture and shadows, but in terms of an interior/exterior juxtaposition that portrays Iago's gradual infiltration and inhabitation of Othello's psyche, his interior self and Othello's fatal flaw, which is his increasing tendency to base judgement on the way things appear on the outside. Like the watery element with which he is affiliated, Iago seeps into Othello's consciousness until he directs his gaze – like a director, leaving the truth on the cutting-room floor. Othello, however, in his search for 'ocular proof' (3.3.365) appears in the film stylistically in terms of exterior shots which often figure silhouetted, back-lit or shadowed characters.

Fig. 7: 'Iago style': Welles' cinematography suggests Iago as a fluid entity

The most prominent juxtaposition of Welles' interior/exterior styles is found in a brief scene set in Othello and Desdemona's chamber. This follows and overlaps a scene in which Iago, in the streets outside, drinks 'happiness to their sheets' (2.3.25), a deviant reiteration of his earlier accusation of Othello's adultery: 'twixt my sheets/He has done my office' (2.1.369–70). This accusation notably contrasts Desdemona's earlier suggestion of purity and virginity: 'Lay on my bed my wedding sheets' (4.2.108) following which she asks Emilia, in the event of her death, to 'shroud me/In one of those same sheets' (4.3.23–4), foreshadowing her own fatal suffocation with a sheet – the handkerchief – at Othello's hands. Symbolically charged with anticipation of Othello's murder of Desdemona in that same chamber, the scene shows Othello and Desdemona's shadows coming together on the wall of the bedroom as Iago looks on from outside and below, suggesting already that his influence has moved from outside to inside and infected Othello's perception.

Mise-en-scène is chiefly important in Welles' production because it operates at all times in conjunction with the play's notion of the fake *mise-en-scène* that Iago constructs for Othello.[1] As a victim of a skewed spectatorship, moreover, Othello's 'false gaze' (1.3.20) draws parallels between Iago's ploy and the cinema spectator who grounds his or her interpretation of a film's narrative in what the *mise-en-scène* reveals. But, asks Welles' film, what about the elements and truths that *mise-en-scène* conceals? The potential deception and potency of this technique are shown on all levels to be fundamental to the effectiveness of Welles' film, and ultimately register the key themes of Shakespeare's play in cinematic terms.

To a similar extent, Almereyda's *Hamlet* deploys the *mise-en-scène* to depict Hamlet as 'observed of all observers' (3.1.153), or as a character imprisoned within a surveillance society that compromises privacy, subjectivity and identity. Almereyda's film crams the *mise-en-scène* with photographs, video images, frames-within-frames and characters dwarfed and reflected by their glassy, postmodern environment to the point that they seem unable to distinguish between substance and reflection. In many ways, the film draws attention to itself as a film by portraying the characters – particularly Hamlet (Ethan Hawke) and Ophelia (Julia Stiles) – as imprisoned behind glass, as though trapped by a camera lens. The entirety of the play is rendered as definitively filmic. Elsinore is, to use Guy Debord's famous term, a 'society of the spectacle' (1995). Accordingly,

Fig. 8: Actor, director, spectator: Hamlet (Ethan Hawke) editing Hamlet

Hamlet's despair is attributed to the suffocating hyperreality of his sur-
roundings. Note the scene in which Hamlet watches a video diary recording of himself holding a gun to his head, grinning, as he says 'To be or
not to be, that is the question'. As he rewinds the scene over and over
again, the camera tracks towards him, eventually revealing his reflection
on the screen superimposing his recorded image, showing in actuality
three Hamlets in one shot: Hamlet the director/editor, viewing and editing
his video diary like a filmmaker; Hamlet the spectator, evidenced by his
reflection on the screen; and Hamlet the actor, performing his own death.
The *mise-en-scène* is crucial in depicting the triangulation and separation
of Hamlet's identity.

With the advent of digital technology it is also possible to contrive
special effects as part of the *mise-en-scène*. Julie Taymor's *Titus*, for example, features what she refers to as 'Penny Arcade Nightmares' (PANs),
or a visual collage composed of computer-generated shots and anima-
tions used 'to portray the inner landscape of the mind as effected by the
external actions' (2000: 183). Occuring five times throughout the film to
heighten the surreal, nightmarish reality endured by the characters, these

sequences usefully (and perhaps forcefully) announce the symbolic layers of the narrative's tragic events. The first PAN registers Tamora's (Jessica Lange) plans to avenge the merciless slaughter of her first-born son at Titus' (Anthony Hopkins) command by showing Tamora and Titus in profile facing each other, Titus at screen right and Tamora at screen left. The positions of the characters in the *mise-en-scène* indicate that Tamora is the figure of action and the character whose point of view we share, as screen movement is normally left to right. Behind these characters is a montage of fire with animated dismembered body parts floating inwards towards the spectator. These are the body parts of Tamora's dead son, still breathing, bleeding and moaning. The sequence both evokes Tamora's anger at her son's murder – the breathing and moving body parts suggesting that, although dead, he is still alive to her – and her vow to take revenge, an act which similarly involves dismemberment.

A second PAN alters the tragic tone of the film, counterpointing Lavinia's (Laura Fraser) memory of her horrific rape and disfigurement by inserting flashes of a symbolically-loaded PAN throughout the scene in which she writes the names of her attackers with a stick in the sand. In the Penny Arcade sequence the scene cuts to a blue-toned shot of Lavinia on a tree stump wearing a white dress that billows upwards, recalling the famous shot of Marilyn Monroe in *The Seven Year Itch* (1955). Immediately Lavinia is paralleled with an icon of feminine sexuality, and subsequently as an innocent victim, as the head of a doe suddenly appears on her shoulders. At either side of Lavinia in the sequence are pouncing tigers – echoing Titus' comment that 'Rome is but a wilderness of tigers' (3.1.53) – upon which appear the heads of Demetrius (Matthew Rhys) and Chiron (Jonathan Rhys Meyers), at once announcing the identities of her attackers and exposing the events of the rape as a symbolic slaughter of innocence. The scene is most effective in articulating Lavinia's enforced silence – as Demetrius and Chiron removed her tongue – and in capturing the surreality of the trauma from Lavinia's point of view, rendering in addition the play's imagery of tigers and the doe.

What these examples indicate is that *mise-en-scène* can be seen as a system of techniques that work in harmony to produce a particular interpretive effect. Specifically, the *mise-en-scène* generates narrative layers which both advance the plot and reveal information about the characters and subtext(s), all of which contributes to our understanding of the overall meaning. In sum, *mise-en-scène* can be described as a machine whose 'cogs' – acting, costume, format, lighting, props, space and setting – function together to generate our perception of the narrative, and to construct the film's forms.

Cinematography

In some ways, it is difficult to tell where cinematography begins and *mise-en-scène* ends. The main difference, as will be considered here, is in terms of camera movement. As a brief example, whether a camera is hand-held, Steadicam or put on a tripod or dolly adds an enormous amount of symbolic currency to the film and, consequently, to the way in which the plot is narrated. Cinematography involves three key areas: framing, lighting and camera movement, in accordance with the responsibilities of a film's cinematographer or Director of Photography (also called a DP or DOP). Translating literally as 'writing in movement', cinematography can be thought of as a mode of writing the film 'text' and engaging with film language, which is another term for film form. In this regard, the camera serves as the pen – or 'caméra-stylo' as Alexandre Astruc put it in 1948 – that composes cinematic texts. Cinema's 'language' that Christian Metz (1974) described is the system of techniques that become possible in telling a narrative or, in other words, a film's style.

In Luhrmann's *Romeo + Juliet*, cinematography is essential to the creation of a definitively postmodern Shakespeare. The film is part of Luhrmann's 'Red Curtain Trilogy', so named to define the 'theatricalised cinematic form' underpinning its three film installments (Andrew 2001). This hybrid form appears in *Romeo + Juliet* and is extrapolated later in *Moulin Rouge!* as a method of staging cinema, or of using 'every cinematic trick we [could] think of to make it look as much like a movie as we [could]' (cinematographer Donald McAlpine, quoted in Hamilton 2002: 163). Cinema in *Romeo + Juliet* is placed centre-stage, predominantly in terms of a highly theatrical, or at times operatic, visual style. The effort to put cinema on display is executed as an energetic montage of historical genres, film styles and media. Photographed by Donald McAlpine, a former documentary cameraman, the film showcases a range of flamboyant camera techniques with newly-coined names such as 'Super Macro Slam Zoom', 'Lightning Cut', 'Chopper POV' (see Pearce & Luhrmann 1996: 9, 152, 154).

As an example from the film will demonstrate, McAlpine's camera is frantically restless, as though 'trying to keep ahead of the audience' (Adamek 1996) and grappling with a transient world.

At times taking on the guise of a news camera in pursuit of a high-speed car chase, the film's cinematography roots us firmly in a latter-day 'meta-city' – 'Verona Beach', filmed here in Mexico City, the world's most populated city, and also in Vera Cruz – that is dense, smoggy and prone to a lot of crime (which affected production, during which the hair and make-up personnel were kidnapped by bandits and only released upon payment of a ransom). Mexico City's dirty, sun-scorched, prostitute-riddled streets were filmed using a hand-held camera. This contributes to the sense of immediacy, as if we were on the streets ourselves. Other camera manoeuvres pick out important iconography amongst the crowded cityscape, and are designed to draw attention to the film's style as entirely different from anything we have ever witnessed in a Shakespeare film before. There is also a noticeable overlap between the film's cinematography and iconography. This is underlined by a coding system that rhythmically and stylistically integrates the cinematography with the film's iconography and characterisation. Says Luhrmann, 'the coding and referencing is to help the audience understand where they are as well as making a new work in itself' (quoted in Andrew 2001). As part of this code, McAlpine's cinematography communicates to audiences the film's historical, geographic, ideological and stylistic references, and also announces its own unique take on Shakespeare's play.

Most of the film's cinematic flamboyance is crammed into the first ten minutes after the credit sequence. Following the double iteration of the prologue – first by an African-American anchorwoman (Edwina Moore) from the confines of an old-style television set against a black backdrop, then by Friar Lawrence's (Pete Postlethwaite) voice-over as a series of montages establish the film's tone and location – the film's title appears, with the iconic cross appearing as a symbolic conjunction between the words 'Romeo' and 'Juliet'. A slow wipe across the screen reveals a shot of three young men in a yellow convertible driving along a freeway. The camera is positioned at the back of the car. A tattoo reading 'Montague' on the back of a bald character's head tells us that these are 'the Montague Boys'. Cutting to a shot of the front of the car (via a version of the iris, a transition mode characteristic of the silent era), the scene suddenly freeze-frames to introduce the characters alongside a caption shot. The use of freeze-frame here conjures Martin Scorsese's iconic mode of 'cinematic exposition in which characters and objects are portrayed in a moment between movement and non-movement' used also to convey 'the importance and possible meaning of each object and functions as a thematic catalyst' (Castellitto 1998: 23). In Luhrmann's film, the image suspension is particularly effective in permitting the spectator to meditate, however briefly, upon the meticulous and deliberately kitschy *mise-en-scène* amongst a flurry of hyperkinetic zooms and transitions, and contributes to the overall rhythm.

Following the freeze-frame of the Montague boys, a quick succession of wipes show two signs, one of which (a billboard) reads '"Retail'd to Posterity" by Montague Construction', a line taken from *Richard III* (3.1.77). The other sign is for Phoenix Gas, the petrol station at which the Montagues arrive. The car pulls into a low-level medium shot – showing the car's registration plate, MON 005, up close – before the camera pulls up in front of the dashboard. A series of medium shots captures each of the three Montague boys before panning to the left into a tight shot of another registration plate, CAP 005. Without cutting, the camera proceeds to travel quickly at ground level to the driver's door, which opens. In true spaghetti western style, we see nothing of the driver except his steel-heeled cowboy boots, which feature the emblem of a cat on the heel. This is also the Capulet logo. Another freeze-frame introduces us to 'the Capulet Boys' and, in a later shot, to the wearer of the cowboy boots – Tybalt, 'Prince of Cats' (John Leguizamo). Significantly, the ground-level travelling shot towards Tybalt sees the camera prowl like a cat, and so anticipates and mimics this character (and the Capulets in general) in terms of a cinematographic motif.

The stand-off between Tybalt and Benvolio Montague (Dash Mihok) is played out as an almost rhythmic sequence of close-up/extreme close-up shots and hand-held medium shots. The action is up close and personal, and heightened by the frequent cuts between shots. Even at this pace, McAlpine speeds up a shot of Tybalt reloading his gun, yet slows down a shot of him performing a flamenco dance move as he shoots at the Montagues and leaps sideways into the air behind his car. Despite the chaotic narrative situation, the pace of the narrative is deliberately and precisely controlled throughout the entire scene. As an example, the rhythm of the camera movements and the types of shots used – extreme

Fig. 9: The Montagues and Capulets set the 'cross' ablaze in *William Shakespeare's Romeo + Juliet* (1996)

close-ups and 'Super Macro Slam Zooms' – alert the viewer to the wealth of religious iconography throughout the scene, such as the embroidered image of Jesus Christ on Tybalt's waistcoat, Abra's back tattoo, the shaven cross on the back of another Capulet's head, the cross symbols on the gun stocks, Abra's cross necklace, the cross shape of Tybalt's gun sight and, significantly, the gas-filled cross shape on the ground into which Tybalt drops a second cigarette, setting the 'cross' on fire. Although the scene itself is packed with action, McAlpine's camera ensures that we never miss the significant aspects or symbols of the narrative.

McAlpine's lighting draws attention to shifts in the tone and to con-nective patterns across the film's visual elements. In particular, the scene after Romeo shoots Tybalt reveals Romeo's dismay at being banished from Verona and, in turn, registers his affiliation with the city. Captured in a close-up shot gazing upward at what is suggested to be a window at night through which moonlight, lightning and rain shine, Romeo begins the scene *in medias res* by responding to news of his enforced exile: 'Banishment? Be merciful, say "death"' (3.3.12). Here an unwashed bloody cut on Romeo's cheek appears glaringly red against the blue light of the window. In reality, the lightning, moonlight and rain are a combination of

McAlpine's minimalist lighting techniques. Using only one light, McAlpine placed it directly above DiCaprio's face and created a 'texture' of light by diffusing it through glass and other materials (including a crucifix pattern), and adding water to the glass (see McAlpine 2006). Strobe lights were used to create lightning effects. The use of a blue-toned filter over the light produces a cold atmosphere, adding to Romeo's banishment and to the declension of tone and pace after Tybalt's death. The use of blue on Romeo's face also foreshadows the blue light emanating from the neon crosses in the church at Juliet's 'funeral', which illuminate Romeo's face as he walks up the aisle towards her. Significantly, in this final scene, banishment is certainly transposed to death.

McAlpine's cinematography is rigorously (and conventionally) connective throughout the film, guiding the spectator to make formal associations between techniques that inform our interpretation of the narrative. The presence of cross imagery in the gas station shoot-out at the beginning, and again at the lovers' death scene towards the end, organises the film's imagery into a recognisable symbolic structure, and keeps the viewer initiated and alert to the multiple layers of the shot.

Editing

Film editing is the process of linking shots together in order to create a narrative sequence. Early Soviet filmmakers called attention to the potential meanings that could arise from two or more juxtaposed shots. But the transition from one shot to another can be achieved in many ways, each of which enables a symbolic dialogue between images. Typically, an edited sequence of shots is seamless, meaning that the editing appears invisible to the viewer. As most of us watch films on a regular basis, we are already accustomed (often without realising it) to continuity editing. Instead of viewing every scene in a wide shot, we are called upon to negotiate a series of close-ups, medium shots, long shots, pans, tracking shots, crane shots and establishing shots, all of which are strung together in sequence to aid us in making sense of what is happening. But editing can also be deliberately discontinuous, either by cutting away to a parallel action in a different time or space, or what David Bordwell and Kristin Thompson refer to as a graphic match (1997: 274–6). This is a cut from one shot to another that connects both shots in terms of their graphic similarity; for instance, the moon slicing across a cloud in *Un Chien Andalou* (1929) to the slicing of a razor over an eyeball. Conversely, conflict can be created between shots by cutting from shot A to shot B, which is completely (or perhaps seemingly) unrelated, such as the occasional insertion of shots of a plane in the sky throughout Almereyda's *Hamlet*, ostensibly indicating Hamlet and Ophelia's desire for escape. As Bordwell and Thompson observe, 'editing permits the filmmaker to relate *any* two points in space through similarity, difference, or development' (1997: 280). The techniques by which this is accomplished contribute much to our understanding of the relationships between shots.

Like many terms pertinent to film style, the term 'editing' covers a number of cutting methods. The reaction shot, shot/reverse shot, point-of-view shot, cutaway, master shot and cross-cutting are all forms of general transitions which create spatial and temporal relations within a scene. Shot transitions are important in bringing a scene to a close, suggesting elapsed time, forging a point of distinction or comparison between one scene and another, or simply adding to the film's narrative rhythm. Transitional techniques include fade-out, which – as the name suggests – involves fading to black (or occasionally to white), the dissolve (the simultaneous co-presence of two overlapping shots) and jump cut (a technique used during the early days of cinema and developed during the French New Wave to render a temporal ellipsis as artificially as possible). A wipe literally wipes the shot off-screen by means of a line moving across the screen, replacing the end shot with the beginning of a new scene that appears behind the wipe line.

Editing can also occur without cutting away from one shot to the next. Baz Luhrmann's use of varying film speeds provides one instance of elliptical editing without cutting away. Film normally runs through a camera at a rate of 24 frames per second (fps). Any manipulation of the shooting speed will affect the image, either in blurry motion (26 to 28 fps) or in fast motion (120 fps). The acceleration of film speed is a transitional device that 'edits' real time without cutting from one shot to another. *Romeo + Juliet* oscillates between slow and fast film speeds, each of which is attributed with particular qualities pertinent to the tone of a scene. Many parts of the film are speeded up apparently to fast-forward past the 'boring bits', as Luhrmann admits, such as a scene in which Juliet's mother persuades her to date Dave Paris (Paul Rudd). As she moves away to put on a Cleopatra costume the film is suddenly fast-forwarded to the more significant part of the scene. 'Who wants to see her put a dress on?' Luhrmann asks. 'But she's got to be in the scene. You can't cut away' (quoted in Adamek 1996). Luhrmann's decision not to cut away keeps the spectator 'rooted' in a shot while taking the liberty of punctuating the most relevant and important sections of the narrative. The use of accelerated speed instead of shot transitions eschews the more conventional methods for techniques that are rigorously postmodern and in keeping with the 'editing' facilities available to the modern viewer.

An earlier Shakespeare appropriation provides a highly-stylised example of classical transition techniques. Akira Kurosawa's first Shakespeare endeavour, *Throne of Blood* (*Kumonosu jô*) is based on *Macbeth*. Set in medieval Japan, the film reprises Kurosawa's interest in Samurai culture by figuring Macbeth/Washizu (Toshiro Mifune) as a feudal lord who is 'murdered by ambition'. Kurosawa's stridently formalist editing of *Throne of Blood* contributes enormously to the aesthetic dynamism of the film. Vertical wipes are used, often making the transition from light to dark palettes, which in turn mark a symbolic journey throughout the film from moral lightness to darkness. At the film's beginning, during which a series of messengers bring news to their *daimyo* about an invasion of North Castle by the Fujimaki, a series of wipes increase the pace of the narrative until we are introduced to Captains Washizu and Miki/Banquo (Minoru Chiaki), who come across a witch in Cobweb Forest. Anticipated by a blinding mist, the witch predicts their fates before disappearing into obscurity. Following this scene, Washizu and Miki's attempt to find their way out of the forest is obstructed by the fog. A series of shots show them galloping from mist-sheathed invisibility towards the camera, silently bewildered. Each shot of the fog dissolves into another, until it appears that the fog is operating as an editing aesthetic. Kurosawa's use of match shots of the fog blend into one another until the spectator fully shares the sense of dislocation and disorientation experienced by Washizu and Miki.

A similar match shot technique appears on several occasions later in the film. When Lady Asaji Washizu/Lady Macbeth (Isuzu Yamada) informs Macbeth that she will offer the guards 'refreshments' as a prelude to their slaughter at Washizu's hands, she is captured from behind, centre-frame, walking through the chamber doors into darkness. As she fades into blackness the camera does not cut away; instead, the darkness of the adjoining room remains in the centre, framed by the two doors. Facing us, Asaji returns from the darkness and walks towards the camera, carrying a large container (for 'refreshments'). By showing Asaji enveloped by shadow instead of cutting away, Kurosawa cleverly insinuates her entrance into moral darkness and her return – carrying the urn-like container – as a murderess.

In other scenes, Kurosawa opens with shots of screens – whether door-screens or curtains – that are pulled back to reveal a subsequent shot. For example, when a servant brings Washizu news of his child's stillbirth, the scene begins with a shot of a closed screen door that is pulled back to reveal Washizu, before whom the servant kneels. A later shot begins with a curtain that Washizu pulls back to reveal Asaji relentlessly washing her hands. Other transitions, such as fade to black, are used precisely to capture moments of closure, and to punctuate a cadence within the narrative's rhythm (such as the fade once Washizu and Miki realise that the witch's predictions have come true). Editing here is an immensely important ingredient not only in organising the film, but in creating character motifs and formal patterns.

Lastly, montage (from the French, meaning 'putting together') is a chief editing principle, but must be noted as discrete from conventional conceptions of film editing. Montage differs from editing insofar as it is often an isolated sequence of rapidly successive shots that generally provide condensed narrative information that occurs over a period of time, or to juxtapose singularly meaningful and unrelated images in order to create a 'third' meaning. A montage experiment carried out by Lev Kuleshov in 1918 revealed the role of the spectator in creating meanings that are not necessarily present in a single shot, or in a series of shots. However, later theorists classified the potential of montage according to its diverse functions. These functions include narrative, expressive, creative, syntactic, semantic and rhythmic (see Aumont *et al.* 1994: 45–52). Whilst these categories are more or less out of date, they nonetheless prove useful in identifying the various possibilities for film montage, and confirm that the montage 'effect' is never the same in any two productions.

Almereyda's *Hamlet* configures the dumb-show used by Hamlet to 'catch the conscience of the king' (2.2.582) as a silent montage sequence of specifically relevant – though not entirely related – images. The shot sequence is as follows:

1. Title Card: red background with white text, reading 'The Mouse-trap' – similar to the film's title card. Three subsequent title cards follow reading 'A Tragedy By', 'Hamlet', 'Prince of Denmark' consecutively. Cut to black.
2. Fade in to a time-lapse shot of a red rose against a blue background coming into bloom.
3. Slow fade to a colour shot of a living room, circa 1950s. A mother and father sit on a sofa as a young boy enters the room. Cut to a medium shot of the characters, situating the little boy between his parents. The father lifts the little boy on the sofa between them.
4. Cut to a black-and-white shot of older footage of a man playing affectionately with a young boy who sits on his knee. Cut to (same footage) father taking his son out of the room, presumably to bed, past his mother who sits in a separate armchair.
5. Cut to Hamlet's audience.
6. Cut back to black-and-white footage of father watching his son climb into bed.
7. Slow fade to a shot of a fake globe, spinning in a fake universe. Fade to black.
8. Quick fade into very old black-and-white footage of a bottle of poison, replete with skull and crossbones label.
9. Slow fade into monochrome footage of cells under a microscope.
10. Cut to a shot over Hamlet and Ophelia's shoulders, watching cell footage, which fades to bottle of poison, then an animation shot of a silhouetted 'hard-boiled' character entering a red room. Hamlet looks over his shoulder past the camera.
11. Cut to Hamlet's POV: Gertrude (Diane Venora) and Claudius (Kyle McLachlan) watch the film from the back. Claudius is perturbed.
12. Cut back to The Mousetrap: an animation of a white-collar man lounging on a chair against a red background.
13. Cut to another animation shot of a hand pouring the contents of a test-tube against a red background. Cut to an extreme close-up of the contents spilling.
14. Cut to an extreme close-up animation of a man's ear, into which the contents pour. A circle emits from the ear, confirming 'impact'.

15. Cut to a medium close-up of Claudius, who visibly gulps.
16. Cut to Hamlet looking over his shoulder at Claudius, then back at the screen.
17. Cut to very old black-and-white footage of a man staggering across the screen, then collapsing.
18. Cut to old black-and-white footage of a theatrical production, presumably *Julius Caesar*, in which Roman guards watch as a man is strangled.
19. Cut back to Claudius, who looks away from the screen towards Hamlet.
20. Cut back to Hamlet, who looks away from Claudius towards the screen. A black-and-white clip shows athletes rhythmically falling forward like dominos.
21. Cut to Marcella (Paula Malcomson) and Horatio (Karl Geary); Horatio looks over his shoulder at Claudius.
22. Cut to Hamlet, looking at Claudius. A psychedelic spiral is on-screen, fading gradually into another time-lapse shot of a rose. This time the rose withers.
23. Cut to black-and-white footage of a little boy in pyjamas at the bottom of stairs.
24. Cut back to theatrical production; a guard kisses the hand of 'Cleopatra'.
25. Cut to a shot from a porn film.
26. Cut to Gertrude's reaction; she is visibly disturbed.
27. Cut to a colour shot of an audience applauding.
28. Cut to Hamlet looking over his shoulder at the King and Queen.
29. Cut to Gertrude's reaction, looking at Hamlet.
30. Cut to old black-and-white footage of a character watching himself in a mirror as he places a very ornate crown on his head. Cut to a frontal shot of the character, nodding and smiling with the crown in place.
31. Cut to Claudius, who rises to his feet.
32. Cut to Hamlet, who sees Claudius and also rises.
33. Cut to audience shot; both Hamlet and Claudius are on their feet. Claudius leaves the theatre, and Hamlet follows him.
34. Cut to Ophelia looking over her shoulder at the activity; a black -and-white title card on the screen reads 'The End'.

This sequence reveals the isolated, connective and expressive registers of Hamlet's montage which, as a whole, depicts the murder of Old Hamlet. Notably, vital elements of Old Hamlet's murder are not revealed: the villain is visible briefly as a silhouetted figure (shot 12) but is never shown to be Claudius. Hamlet's video-diary footage would easily have provided direct images of Claudius for insertion into the montage, but instead Hamlet chooses to imply Claudius' involvement. Shots of cells, blooming or withering roses, and porn actors seem indicative in themselves of the decay of love and innocence, and the union of Gertrude and Claudius as pornographic. In juxtaposition with other shots, however, these images indicate the effects of poison, death and adultery. And these images represent the Shakespearean text, visualising respectively the 'quintessence of dust' (2.2.298) of which man is composed, the dichotomy of 'to be or not to be' (3.1.58), and the 'rank sweat of an enseamèd bed' (3.4.81) created by Claudius and Gertrude's marriage.

As a reflection of another narrative, Hamlet's montage – here a film within a film – is entirely indexical; that is, its images consistently refer not only to each other but to an extratextual event. The motif of the circle (shots 7, 9, 14 and 22, as well as the cover design for the Mousetrap's programme) is vital in signifying the concentric circles that compose the montage's symbolic radius. In its entirety, the montage is organised as a series of shots that do not progress symbolically or otherwise in a linear fashion, but as a series of circles moving inwards – approximately towards the psychedelic spiral pattern in shot 22. That is to say, the shots each spiral potential meanings that resonate with each of the other shots individually and collectively, creating a host of connective patterns: rather like the domino-effect produced by the falling athletes in shot 20. The juxtaposition of shots 2, 3 and 4, for instance, construct a mini-montage that suggests the bloom of youth and innocence, and of paternal love. The juxtaposition of shots 3 and 24 overturns the earlier portraits of familial stability, whilst shots 7 and 9 correspond in terms of a contrasting macrocosmic/microcosmic 'zoom' from Hamlet's consideration of man 'like a god' to a 'quintessence of dust' (2.2.296, 298). Perhaps more importantly, however, the 'gaps' in Hamlet's montage are precisely what probes Claudius' guilt. What is not depicted in the montage is just as important as what *is*.[2]

In sum, film editing is the organisation of single-shot units into a meaningful structure. An important element in film narration – that is, in reporting or presenting the narrative – editing is the key stylistic ingredient in creating a formal cause/effect narrative pattern, in engaging the spectator with the film's formal characteristics and in making an otherwise unintelligible or confused film coherent and appealing. As Valerie Orpen says, 'editing can "save" or maim a film' (2003: 7). As a host of films under the sub-category 'Director's Cut' attest, there is a fair element of struggle between studio and directorial 'versions', usually in terms of film length and content which, as in the case of *Blade Runner* (1982), may alter major narrative strands and reconfigure a film's tone, characterisation and reception. However, it is important to understand editing as entirely cooperative with other elements of film style. Our interpretation of a scene may be affected to a greater extent by the *mise-en-scène*, cinematography or indeed sound, yet our interpretation of the film overall can be greatly determined by the editing patterns throughout.

Sound

Turning the sound off when watching a film is perhaps the best way to appreciate its impact on our engagement with and interpretation of a scene. Although we have paid much attention to film's visual elements so far, sound is an extremely important aesthetic device – if not as important as the image – and has always been so, even during cinema's silent era.[3] The term 'sound' covers a variety of sub-categories, including speech, music and noise or sound effects (Bordwell & Thompson 1997: 320). It is not always clear which of these categories a particular sound falls into, as the post-production creation of the sound of an action is often the result of an entirely unrelated acoustic process (such as the whooshing hail of arrows at Agincourt in Olivier's *Henry V*, created by a technician moving a willow switch one hundred times in front of a microphone). Sound in a film can also be diegetic (happening within the story, for example a radio that a character turns on/off) or non-diegetic (outside the narrative world). In principle, if a character can hear the sound, it is diegetic; if not, it is non-diegetic. Perhaps just as important as sound is the use of silence – in building suspense, in contributing to the film's tone, adding to dramatic impact or inviting the viewer to pay attention to the imagery. The quality, timbre, volume, pitch, tone and texture of sound in a scene generate massive amounts of narrative information and a significant quantity of sub-textual detail.

The beginning of Richard Loncraine's *Richard III* serves as a compelling example of the effective use of film sound. After a number of red title cards giving plot information are superimposed upon a black screen, the loud rattling of a ticker tape machine is heard alongside a close-up of its message: 'Richard Gloucester is at hand: he holds his course toward Tewkesbury.' Immediately, the film's situation – war – and historical setting are announced by the use of ticker tape and its message. We then cut to two army generals (James Dreyfus and David Antrobus) who read the transcript and bid each other goodnight, calling each other 'father' and 'son'. The following scene – in which the younger general enjoys an evening meal and a glass of red wine while his dog chews at a bone – creates massive suspense without any dialogue at all. The accentuated sound of the pouring wine, as well as the eating and chewing sounds, lead up to a low rumbling sound that prompts the general to shush the ticker tape operator in the background. Suddenly, an army tank bursts through the wall and masked soldiers spill from its insides, shooting the general and his team dead. As the camera centralises on one of the masked soldiers, heavy, rhythmic breathing, as though through the gas-mask, punctuates the soundtrack. A series of low brass orchestral chords add to the sinister tone of the scene. As the masked soldier stomps into the chamber of the older general – King Edward in the play, who is shown here at prayer – the noise of the soldier's breathing and footsteps are counterpointed by rhythmic gun shots that continue after he lowers his gun and removes his gas-mask. At this point the film's title fills the screen in large red letters that appear one by one in time with the gun shots, covering Richard's (Ian McKellen) unmasked face and echoing into the distance.

That one sound overlaps another in this sequence is significant in the film's successful construction of rising suspense and, more importantly, characterisation, in a very short space of time. Each of the sounds circulate around the main character: the ticker tape announces his arrival, the sound of the dog eating a bone insinuates Richard's bestiality whilst the sound of the pouring wine invokes the blood sacrifice he is about to make. Likewise, the ostinato of the approaching tank reprises the tapping of the ticker tape, suggesting his imminent approach as though from the bowels of the earth, 'sent before [his] time/Into this world' (1.1.20–1) not from his mother's womb as in the play, but from the womb of hell. The sound of the tank bursting through the wall is like an explosion, pre-empting Richard's explosive forcefulness to the top of the monarchy. The breathing sounds through the mask, coupled with shots of Richard's point of view, insert the spectator 'inside' his mask, preparing us for the way in which he will invite us to share his subjectivity and murderous plans throughout the film. The breathing also establishes Richard's character long before we hear him speak by referencing (yet again) Darth Vader. The one-two rhythm of the gun-shot title appearing on screen picks up Richard's pulse-like breathing, suggesting his monstrosity and (intimidating) proximity to both the film's characters and, ostensibly, its spectators.

Sound also serves to create deeper conceptual registers in a film, many of which cannot be presented visually in full. In Almereyda's *Hamlet*, the recurrent use of voice-over works in tandem with Hamlet's narcissistic habit of watching himself on screen to suggest what Michel Chion describes as the disembodied voice, or 'acousmatic voice', which relates to sound without discernible origins (1999: 27). In this production, Hamlet's saturation in images and mediated representations of the real suggests his displacement from reality and, indeed, from his own origins, his sense of self. Upon deeper reflection of the voice-over's theoretical pronouncements, it is arguable that sound is used in this film to articulate the Oedipal undertones of Hamlet's character in different and more complex ways to previous productions, perhaps in keeping with the film's postmodern appropriation of *Hamlet*. In Francesco Casetti's opinion, the voice-over 'serves as a kind of umbilical cord: it ties us to something we have lost, it puts us on the trail of a presence that has been taken away' (1999: 238). Furthermore, Mary Ann Doane connects the voice in cinema to primary experiences of the *maternal* voice, the voice of 'the irretrievably lost object of desire' (1999: 371). In this version of *Hamlet*, the lost object of desire is not entirely the mother, but instead the sense of a real, concrete world that has been replaced by representation. The 'trail of a presence' here leads only to absence.

In other productions, the soundtrack is important in making extra-diegetic connections and intertextual references. More generally, a film's soundtrack establishes the mood or tone of the production, and can often influence our interpretation of the action. In Olivier's *Henry V*, the light-hearted orchestral soundtrack featuring soft, rising flute motifs downplays the seriousness and reality of war, which effectively asserts Olivier's rousing call to arms during World War II. In Kenneth Branagh's *Love's*

Labour's Lost, the soundtrack plays an integral part in establishing the film's genre, which is a reprisal of the 1930s' Hollywood musical. Patrick Doyle's soundtrack also co-ordinates with the film, often interacting with and mimicking the pitch of *a capella* song numbers, and responding to the rhythm of dance moves. Returning once more to Luhrmann's *Romeo + Juliet*, however, we can see that the pop soundtrack serves to situate the film firmly in MTV culture and often parodies the music video aesthetic. The familiarity of Luhrmann's aesthetic to contemporary audiences makes Shakespeare familiar and accessible. The soundtrack compensates for the Shakespearean language employed throughout the film, often using lyrics to explain particularly challenging parts of the text. Think of Radiohead's 'Talk Show Host' (1996) during the scene in which a melancholic Romeo writes in his diary the words: 'heavy lightness, serious vanity,/Misshapen chaos of well-seeming forms' (1.1.171–2). Here, Radiohead's lyric provides a contemporary understanding of Romeo's notes: 'I want to be someone else or I'll explode/Floating upon the surface for/The birds.' Likewise, Des'ree's 'Kissing You' (1996) – performed during the meeting scene between Romeo and Juliet – provides an alternative context for Juliet's comment, 'you kiss by th' book' (1.5.107):

Watching stars without you my soul cried
Heaving heart is full of pain
Oh, oh, the aching
'Cause, I'm kissing you oh
I'm kissing you oh
Touch me deep, pure and true gift to me forever
'Cause, I'm kissing you.

As these examples demonstrate, sound and music serve many purposes. Sound often works in co-operation with a film's visual qualities to generate modes of interpretation, as a method of characterisation, to heighten, underscore or anticipate the action, or to reveal deeper conceptual ideologies. Like other elements of film which depend on technical equipment, sound is only as effective as technology allows. Early classical films were limited to microphones that required the actors to deliver their lines quite close to the camera, and, until around 1946, sound recording instruments were so bulky (and cameras so noisy) that dialogue was dubbed in post-production (see Monaco 1981: 99). In its various guises – whether voice-over, effects or soundtrack motifs – sound is important in detailing characterisation, in adding to the film's metaphoric allusions and subtexts and in developing the narrative. We normally assume a film's sound to be occurring in real time but, as voice-over and sonic manipulations show us, the use of echoes and other motifs can foreshadow or symbolically re-present various layers of the film's time. In this regard, film music proves a potent device, creating intertextual connections or serving as a metonymic symbol of a particular film (such as the theme tune to *Gone With the Wind* (1939) or the shark motif in *Jaws* (1975)). As emergent developments in film technology and home cinema attest, sound is a fundamental element of film, and contributes in diverse ways to our experience of a production.

Conclusions

Film style covers a broad terrain of aesthetic elements which continue to increase with the advent of many new technologies, trends and evolving industrial conditions. Although I have tried to examine as many formal characteristics as possible (particularly the key players), other areas worth considering include film format, focal lengths and types of shot, conti-nuity, colour, types of lighting, perspective, aspect ratio and framing. A notable example of the last of these is Oliver Parker's *Othello* (1995), in which cinematographer David Johnson's framing techniques create what Patricia Dorval (2000) observes as 'threshold aesthetics' by consistently framing characters, shots and scenes within doorways and thresholds. Taking the play's depiction of Iago as a Janus-faced character – and from there the idea of Janus as the mythical guardian of doorways and thresh-olds – Johnson folds this threshold motif into his cinematography as a recurrent framing device. In studying Shakespeare on film, one of the chief reasons for exploring film style is to comprehend the ways in which the Shakespearean text is transposed and, more exactly, how it can facilitate particular aesthetic innovations – as Parker's film demonstrates – that revitalise *both* a formal technique and the preoccupations of the text.

Economic and industrial limitations have been noted here, yet it is also important to acknowledge limitations that cannot always be categorised, much less anticipated. Suffice it to say that a filmmaker will always be called upon to make compromises and improvisations by factors beyond his or her control, such as bandits and hurricanes in the case of Baz Luhrmann, lack of studio support as in the case of Welles and Almereyda, or, as the following example shows, location problems. Sidney Lumet says:

> I once asked Akira Kurosawa why he had chosen to frame a shot in *Ran* [1985] in a particular way. His answer was that if he'd panned the camera one inch to the left, the Sony factory would be sitting there exposed, and if he'd panned an inch to the right, we would see the airport – neither of which belonged in a period movie. Only the person who's made the movie knows what goes into the decisions that result in any piece of work. (1995: ix)

Although Lumet's comment is not intended to deny the symbolic currency of Kurosawa's cinematography, it does indicate the variety of factors in choosing to shoot a film a particular way. Yet those factors governing a film's production do not (and should not) necessarily affect the entirety of its reception. Film style involves the interaction not only of a host of formal devices and their corresponding factors but their interactions with the film's spectators as well, who ultimately must make sense of the way the film 'looks' to them.

4   POPULARISATION

A 2002 episode of the American television sitcom *My Wife and Kids* (2001–05) provides a glance at the popularisation of Shakespeare in contemporary culture.[1] In this episode the show's female lead, Mrs Kyle (Tisha Campbell), ambitiously leads a group of five-year-olds in a performance of *Romeo and Juliet*. After she falls ill, Mrs Kyle's husband (Damon Wayans) is assigned to her teaching post. When one of the young students asks him to explain the meaning of 'what light through yonder window breaks' (2.1.44), Mr Kyle explains 'That means "Yo, the sun is out"'. Reluctant to perform Shakespeare at all, the children settle on an updated version of the play called 'Romeo and Juliet: The Final Conflict', an amalgamation of Shakespeare, *Jack and the Beanstalk*, *Crouching Tiger, Hidden Dragon* (2000) and *The Omen III: The Final Conflict* (1981). At the balcony scene, ninjas and a Jackie-Chan lookalike creep up on Romeo. A 'shark' appears to attack Juliet at her balcony. Whilst Mrs Kyle gets more and more embarrassed in the audience, the children remark enthusiastically, 'this is going great'. Romeo sword-fights the ninjas, and Mr Kyle appears as Cyclops. Recalling a famous scene from *Scarface* (1983), Romeo concludes the production by aiming a (water)gun at Mr Kyle, exclaiming, *à la* Al Pacino as Tony Montana, 'Say hello to my little friend'.

The reconfiguration of *Romeo and Juliet* in this episode as a parodic conflation of recognisable characteristics of popular culture indicates one of the ways in which Shakespeare is being performed in the twenty-first century. Pitted in the episode alongside a fairytale, a cross-cultural film enterprise, a cult horror film, a cult thriller, as well as characters reminiscent of Steven Spielberg's *Jaws*, *The Teenage Mutant Ninja Turtles* (1990) and Jackie Chan, Shakespeare is called upon as a figure of 'high culture' that, ironically and for obvious comic value, is appropriated by kindergarten kids. More importantly, the translation of his text into local dialogue demonstrates a transposition from high to popular (or 'low') culture. Yet in its presentation of the multiple dialogues that occur between elements of 'low' culture, or popular entertainment, and the figurehead of high culture, the kindergarten performance does not entirely shatter the boundaries of conventionality. By choosing *Romeo and Juliet* – and not one of the lesser-known plays like *The Two Noble Kinsmen* or *Cymbeline* – the television episode noticeably avails of previous renditions and symbolisations of the play already in popular circulation, in particular Luhrmann's *Romeo + Juliet* six years previously, and also banks upon the prevalence of the play in high school curricula. What is being recounted in this episode is *not* 'Shakespeare' per se, but Shakespeare as both a major component within a massive network of intertextual dialogues and as the global icon of literacy, intertextuality and culture.

This chapter seeks to address some of the ways in which Shakespeare continues to be made popular in the twenty-first century. Although too numerous to account for in detail within a single chapter, the far-ranging methods and associated contexts of popularisation include globalisation, consumerism, exploitation, digital culture, various aspects of film production and marketing, mass media, tourism, Shakespeare festivals, Shakespeare criticism, the work of particular directors, a very long list of appropriational methods and the vagaries of postmodernism. Central to each of these contexts are several fundamentals, which will form the focus of this chapter: the question, 'is it Shakespeare?', and Shakespeare as a 'bridge' between popular culture and high culture. Shakespeare's dual relationship with popular culture and high culture is problematised by methods of dislocating the Bard from his historical and textual origins in order to fulfil particular cultural agendas. In the films looked to in this chapter, Billy Morrissette's *Scotland, PA* and Tim Blake Nelson's *O*, Shakespeare is not faithfully incarnated but cited, signified and used to vocalise and legitimate particular twenty-first-century cultural concerns. By considering the methods used to popularise Shakespeare in these productions, as well as their respective meditations on what Shakespeare 'means' to popular culture, we shall demonstrate Shakespeare's commodification and appearance in multiple 'pop' contexts as a helpful lens through which to understand the development and organisation of that elusive term, 'culture'.

Before so doing, however, it seems appropriate to overview briefly the history of Bardic popularisation.

Chronicling the Bard in 'popular' culture

Both praised and criticised for his inventive use of imitation and citation of other works during his writing career, Shakespeare's post-mortem popularity has aptly been ensured by appropriations and citations of his works. Barbara Murray (2005) notes 17 adaptations of Shakespeare between 1682 and 1778 which added pessimism and overtones of social despair to plays like *Titus Andronicus*, *Richard II*, *Henry VI* and *Cymbeline* to address the Popish Plot and Exclusion Crisis during the period. Nahum Tate's happy-ending appropriation of *King Lear* occupied the stage for over 150 years, and William Davenant staged *The Tempest* in 1667 as an opera with surprisingly sophisticated special effects. By the eighteenth century, the variety of Shakespeare citations and re-presentations across emerging social strata had generated a substantial public following and cultural eminence.

This is demonstrated by a single historic event. In September 1769, Shakespearean thespian David Garrick organised a three-day Shakespeare 'Jubilee' in Stratford-upon-Avon in celebration of the Bard. Plagued by rain and omitting to utter or perform a single word from Shakespeare's works, Garrick's first Jubilee nonetheless celebrated Shakespeare's cultural status – in particular his representation of English identity – by erecting a statue of the Bard, reciting a public 'Ode to Shakespeare', and by hosting a range of entertainments including fireworks, horse racing and a Grand Parade of characters from Shakespeare's plays (see Babcock 1964). Regarded by historians as the starting point of the Shakespeare 'trade', the Jubilee was also apparently the 'point at which Shakespeare stopped being regarded as an increasingly popular and admirable dramatist, and became a god' (Deelman 1964: 7; see also Hodgdon 1998). With Bard-themed souvenirs on sale at the Jubilee and the first steps taken towards what is now the seat of Shakespeare tourism, it would seem that Shakespeare became not only a 'god' at this event but also a highly marketable commodity.

Yet, as Douglas Lanier observes, Shakespeare's 'un-popularisation' commenced towards the end of the nineteenth century largely with the canonisation of his works and his centralisation within universities as a subject worthy of academic study (2002: 21–49). Throughout literary circles, a scholarly reverence for Shakespeare circulated amongst the Romantics, who highlighted the Bard's apparent 'universality' and 'every-man' quality. With biographies and close textual analyses of the plays emerging throughout this century, a cultural backlash was summed up in George Bernard Shaw's famous phrase in 1901: 'So much for Bardolatry!' (1931: xxxi). Coining the term 'bardolatry' to describe the religious 'wor-ship' of Shakespeare, Shaw's denouncement of the Bard merely added to the escalating belief in Shakespeare's cultural authority. Already appropri-ated, cited and alluded to across a variety of popular forms – including overtures, operas, ballets, paintings, poetry, novels, musicals, as well as other plays – Shakespeare had reached his apex in the mass media just over three hundred years after his death, serving simultaneously to mark the zenith of 'high' culture.

Towards the end of the twentieth century and the beginning of the twenty-first, both the persona of Shakespeare and his works are increas-ingly encountered through various sites of popular culture: as a logo on retail goods ('Shakespeare's Pies' in Australia is a leading franchise) and credit cards (as the silver marker of authenticity); on British postage stamps; as the figurehead of an important tourist location (Stratford-upon-Avon); in *The Simpsons* (1989–present); as the inspiration behind the persona of the frontman of the punk band the Sex Pistols, Johnny Rotten; business management textbooks; and in comic strips. It is in cinema, however, that cultural activity with Shakespeare is at its most diverse. In *The Street King*, for instance, Shakespeare's *Richard III* is re-written to register the problems faced by Hispanic teenagers in contemporary California. *Deliver Us From Eva* (2003) stages an imaginatively reconfigured version of *The Taming of the Shrew* to identify particular ethnic *dis*awareness in Hollywood films, particularly the romantic comedy genre, whilst *Macbeth: The Comedy* (2001) and *Maqbool* (2003) situate *Macbeth* in generically specific contexts that prioritise the cultural revision of Shakespeare's texts.

These films show that Shakespeare's continued popularity cannot be attributed in isolation to the 'universality' or quality of his plays. In short, the level of cultural activity that has surrounded Shakespeare's texts for hundreds of years has imposed meanings upon the plays that perpetuate and alter throughout popular culture. Moreover, the figure of Shakespeare

Fig. 10: Calvin and Hobbes do *Hamlet*

serves at different levels and periods of popular culture to popularise social contexts. For example, Terence Hawkes (1992) has argued at length that Shakespeare's fame during the eighteenth and nineteenth centuries was the product of political attempts to bolster the British Empire's claim as a cultural authority and, ultimately, as a superior nation (see also Swain 1997). A number of historical texts and events evidence Shakespeare's value as national 'property'. During the 1916 Shakespeare Tercentary in Germany, for instance, a 'bizarre struggle between England and Germany' arose 'for possession of Shakespeare as a "national poet"' (Habicht 2001: 443). At an earlier Tercentary (1896), German cultural nationalists claimed Shakespeare as *'unser* [our] Shakespeare', the 'third German classic' alongside Goethe and Schiller (Habicht 2001: 444). A sonnet in Israel Gollancz's book, *A Book of Homage to Shakespeare* (1916), identifies Shakespeare's birth as mythically occurring within English soil: 'Gentle Will Shakespeare, [England's] authentic son,/Wombed in her soul and with her meadows one' (Gollancz 1916: 248; see also Kahn 2001: 460)'.

The romantic depiction of Shakespeare as a mythic figure of Englishness specifically claims the Bard as the progenitor of England's cultural prowess, as the natural 'son' of England and the summation of the virtues of the English character. Shakespeare's popularisation in this context is clearly an attempt to redefine national identity.

Shakespeare's popularisation does not lie in national concerns entirely. Other factors, including technology, reception, shifts in industrial modes of film production, the logic of late capitalism, evolving dynamics of 'politically-correct' representation and cross-cultural dialogues can be seen as motivating Shakespeare's perpetuation throughout popular culture. Beyond these motivating factors, however, are the ramifications of popularising Shakespeare's works. In making Shakespeare 'popular', there has been a tendency in recent films to update and strip down Shakespeare's language, replace the title, boil down the plot and ultimately use the Shakespeare play as a stamp of cultural legitimacy rather than a faithfully-rendered early-modern text. Some critics have viewed this tendency as 'dumbing down' Shakespeare (see Taylor 1990; Bristol 1996). On the other hand, however, attempts to unmoor Shakespeare from the exclusive realms of high culture and launch him into popular spheres have some positive consequences. The 'Shakespeare' films previously mentioned demonstrate the ways in which culturally specific issues like teen drug abuse, high school shootings, racial tensions and ethnic identities are vocalised through the Bardic text. By using Shakespeare as a globally-recognisable framework through which to view and comprehend such diverse issues, these 'unfaithful' popular appropriations forge connections between two disparate historical positions and their respective popular contexts that identify Shakespeare, as Lanier succinctly puts it, as a 'Will for the people' (2006).

That is not to say, however, that all popular appropriations can be viewed in these rather black-and-white terms. Indeed, many efforts have been put forward to identify the various categories of popularisation and appropriation amongst contemporary Shakespeare films, including John C. Tibbetts' identification of a 'mousetrap' method in several recent productions that 'do not adapt [the] plays so much as they assimilate them into their primary texts' (2002: 207). Also at issue is the ways in which Shakespeare is used in these productions, and in various other forms of pop culture. Alan Sinfield observes the use of Shakespeare in some television advertisements to create an association with 'heritage, class status, intelligence, or artistic quality with their products' (quoted in Lanier 2002: 55). In two recent 'Shakespeare' films, *Rave Macbeth* (2001) and *A Midsummer Night's Rave* (2002), Shakespeare is posited as the 'mainstream' entity that reinforces the 'anti-authoritarian' ideology of rave culture. There is neither effort in these films to replace Shakespeare's language with rave music nor any real attempt to transpose Shakespeare's characters or setting to that of the rave. Instead, what is being offered is the juxtaposition of and struggle between rave as a subculture arena and Shakespeare as the 'location' of high culture. In some ways, the rave is a departure from the number of relatively recent 'high school' Shakespeare films and is aimed at a similar teen audience.[2] The use of Shakespeare, therefore, is intended to reach a target audience at the same time as the anti-authoritarian ideology of rave culture is underlined, celebrated and rendered legitimate.

Whilst a host of examples would be necessary to indicate all the different uses of Shakespeare in the popular vicinity, it may be said that, for better or worse, Shakespeare enables overlaps between popular culture and high culture, bestowing upon low-budget, low-culture productions such as Lloyd Kaufmann's fiercely irreverent *Tromeo and Juliet* (1996), or student films like *Star Wars: Macbeth* (1998), a certain amount of aesthetic elevation, cultural authentication, or simply global recognition – much in the same way that an obscure Chinese film suddenly springs up on Western screens once the name 'Quentin Tarantino' is attached.[3] What this obvious disparity alerts us to is to the range of meanings attributed to the terms 'popular culture' and 'high culture'. The word 'popular' means 'people', deriving from the Latin *popularis*, meaning 'for the people'. In its current usage, however, 'popular' does not refer to *all* people; just the majority. For instance, popular entertainment is generally available to the masses, and tends to be thought of as 'low' as it is usually affordable, unsophisticated and plugged into the mainstream. Popular culture is often regarded as the 'other' to high culture, which conversely refers to an exclusive minority. As John Storey observes, high culture was the result of 'the selective appropriation by elite social groups of aspects of what had been until then a shared public culture [and] certain features in the development of the cultural movement we think of as modernism' (2003: 32). Put another way, the boundaries of high culture are drawn around particular cultural objects claimed by an educated elite. A popular icon during the Renaissance, Shakespeare's canonisation and subsequent absorption by academia in the nineteenth century effectively withdrew him from his original 'populist' standing and placed him within the ranks of high-culture exclusivity. Although adaptors and performers continued to revise and alter the plays, the plays' historical, linguistic and textual elements were largely protected from the perils of updating and, indeed, from 'dumbing down' the new scholarly-revered Bard. That Shakespeare is gradually being restored to the people as a popular figure – meaning that his texts are both accessible by all levels of society and saturated with contemporary issues – suggests a return to his original position as a definitively collaborative, urban-based author whose plays are available for public consumption.

As the notion of Shakespeare as an authenticating agent – or a symbol of cultural legitimacy – attests, Shakespeare is not only popularised but also serves to popularise. It is in this light that two case studies are considered in this chapter, with a view to examining the discrete cultural identities and ideologies that Shakespeare articulates in the popular imagination. In *O*, for example, attention is drawn to racial tensions within a US high school, and the culmination of these tensions in the deaths of several students. Delayed release because of the shootings at Columbine High School in Colorado, the film's presentation of teen violence and racism seemed at the time an uncanny, yet timely, reflection of social undercurrents. As I will go on to demonstrate, Shakespeare plays a significant role in both this tragic event and Blake Nelson's adaptation. In Morrissette's *Scotland, PA*, the juxtaposition of Shakespeare and the fast-food industry points up the importance of marketing and manufacturing Shakespeare's 'meaning', at the same time as the logic of the logo figures in this film to underscore Shakespeare's usage as a corporate marker. What these arguments reveal is that, unlike Shakespeare's empty grave at Holy Trinity, the Bard's cultural 'tomb' is filled with the afterlives of many competing viewpoints and ideologies.

What ish my 'Shakespeare'?

An Irish character named Captain McMorris in Shakespeare's *Henry V* asks the question, 'what ish my nation?' (3.2.61–2). This question denotes McMorris' ambivalence about his national identity and, in the play's historical context, his acknowledgement that he is fighting for the enemy. The use of 'ish' instead of 'is', apparently to suggest McMorris' accent, also underlines his ambivalence: is he British or Irish? Keeping the imperialist resonances of this remark in mind, McMorris' comment not only articulates the Irish question but also registers the issue of what constitutes a Shakespeare film. Are irreverent 'low' culture productions to be considered 'Shakespeare' films alongside faithful 'high' culture productions, or do we encounter Shakespeare on film by degrees? Can the use of Shakespeare in popular appropriations register more far-ranging cultural ambivalences? How far do 'high culture' productions ignore these issues in favour of staying true to the original text? More generally, we have to consider as far as possible *what* Shakespeare is – or in film terms, what he means to Hollywood – before identifying whether a film can be deemed 'Shakespeare' or not.

Both this issue and the national registers of McMorris' comment appear in Morrissette's independent film *Scotland, PA*. Taking the alternative title of Shakespeare's *Macbeth*, 'The Scottish Play', as its inspiration, *Scotland, PA* reinvents the subject of *Macbeth* as a geographical site that is, as the film's title suggests, not Shakespeare's original location. Scotland, Pennsylvania (or PA for short) is pointedly the American version of Scotland, UK, its 'sequel' in fact. Shot in Nova Scotia, Canada (after the Latin for 'New Scotland'), *Scotland, PA* imaginatively switches the play's location to its colonial 'sequel', which was founded in the nineteenth century by Scottish immigrants and, as Mark Thornton Burnett notes, conjures the memory of Scotland in Morrissette's production (2005: 194). The film's play on Scotland and Scottish identity seems to suggest, in departure from McMorris' remark, that *Macbeth* is not strictly 'Scottish' either – or at least that the definition of 'Scottish' is up for grabs.

Reconfigured as a black comedy, *Scotland, PA* does away with Shakespeare's language, title, period, politics, genre and (obviously) its geographical location, and sets about re-assembling these displaced features in the form of signifiers, icons and citations. For example, Birnam Wood appears as both an actual forest park and as a fashion motif, captured by the pattern of black, leafless trees that adorns Lady Macbeth's outfit. As with the film's other symbols and citations, the Birnam Wood pattern serves to displace and transfer the play's meaning to a secondary figure. The witches in the play claim that 'Macbeth shall never vanquished be until/Great Birnam wood to high Dunsinane Hill/Shall come against him' (4.1.108–10). In the film, Macbeth is vanquished by the *representation* of that territory, which is embodied (or adorned) by his wife. The film's series of citations and representations indicate Shakespeare as a signifier whose identity is constantly deferred and displaced by the logos, signs and franchises of popular culture.

Taking the advent of the burger industry as its thematic interest, the film is motivated by the question: what if Lord and Lady Macbeth were alive in 1975? Naturally, it seems, they would be a couple of married 'underachievers' flipping burgers in smalltown USA. Macbeth here is Joe McBeth (James LeGros) commonly known as 'Mac'; Lady Macbeth is Pat McBeth (Maura Tierney). Tired of working at Duncan's burger bar, Pat coerces Mac to do away with its owner, Norm Duncan (James Rebhorn) when he overlooks the McBeths and names his new managers as Malcolm (Tom Guiry) and Donald (Geoff Dunsworth) – his two sons. After a visit from three prophesying hippies (instead of witches) named Stacey (Amy Smart), Hector (Timothy 'Speed' Levitch) and Jesse (Andy Dick), Mac takes action and accidentally tips Norm head first into a fat of sizzling french-fry oil. As the burger bar's new owners, Mac and Pat revamp the place as a fast-food joint with a drive-through pickup and intercom service. Meanwhile, staunch vegetarian Detective Ernie McDuff (Christopher Walken) leads an investigation into the murders. More heads roll, until at last the McBeths receive their fates and McDuff – in a nice twist – inherits the fast-food restaurant, which he transforms into the 'home of the garden burger'.

Warmly received at the 2001 Sundance Film Festival, the film has generally been discussed as a vanity project that opportunistically figures Shakespeare's play without paying full attention to the discursive politics of adapting the Bard or to the Shakespeare cultural 'machine' (see Ebert 2002; Hoberman 2002). Yet the lengthy spiel of background information on the film's website and DVD suggests otherwise. By carefully weighing up the film's investments in notions of nationalism, popular culture and textuality, as well as readings of and prior appropriations of *Macbeth*, it is possible to perceive a much more critically aware production that registers much about 'what' Shakespeare is – or means – in the twenty-first century.

The film's juxtaposition of Shakespeare and fast food is an attempt to create a satirical interaction between two signifiers of high and low culture. Punning consistently on 'Mac', Morrissette finds and elaborates upon relationships between the play's title, the commonality of Scottish surnames beginning with this pre-fix, the title of a 1970s' TV show, *McCloud* (1970–77), and the global 'home' of fast food, McDonald's. More exactly, Morrissette is commenting upon and reacting to Shakespeare's 'exploitation' – or what Richard Burt (2002) calls 'Shakesploitation' – by mass media. 'He's everywhere', reads the film's press kit. 'Batman comic books, the Cosby Show, pop music, pornography, films – both direct versions of the plays and adaptations – foreign appropriations: India, Japan, Norway' (Morrissette 2002). 'And', claims Morrissette, 'since the beginning of film it has always been thus'.

The film's press kit identifies cinema as the main harbinger of Shakespeare's popularity. Going on to overview appropriations of Shakespeare's works from cinema's beginning, *Macbeth* in particular, the press kit identifies Shakespeare's contemporary function 'as a kind of social bra' – that is, hoisting up the concerns of the social elite. In departure from a family of films that offer conventionally 'uplifting' retakes of the plays (Olivier's *Henry V* is given as one example), *Scotland, PA* is suggested as part of a breed of 'new Shakespeares' which 'reflect both a felt need for social and cultural anchors and a willingness to re-examine or even to challenge the received wisdom as to just what "Shakespeare" is and means' (ibid.). In order to do so, Morrissette admits the necessity for 'hybrid and socially complex' treatments of the Bard and, for American audiences, the necessity of shedding insecurities about the fact that the British early-modern Bard can 'speak' to the contemporary US spectator. With this in mind, Morrissette attempts to create a 'midground' Shakespeare that 'doesn't shove Shakespeare in people's faces' (ibid.). The attempt to both 'anchor' Shakespeare as a site of meaning and disengage him from stale hermeneutic positions is an ambitious one, but one that the film manages to pull off. This is achieved in part by satirically re-inventing the play's political dimensions to address the timely 'power struggles' of the market economy, specifically those 'found in the intrigues of corporate sabotage, patent stealing, copyright infringement, inside trading and stock manipulation' (ibid.). By imagining the creation of a 'McBeth with cheese', or a Shakespearean McDonald's, the film figures a 'drive-thru' Shakespeare, or a Shakespeare who is packaged and sold as a fast-food product, the 'taste' of which is decidedly homogeneous. In short, this repackaged 'drive-thru'

Shakespeare is boiled-down and battered-up not by fringe films or promiscuous off-shoots, but by those conventional productions that, one way or another, bend to the will of the global marketplace and offer up the 'same' old Bard: the 'same' as the play, or the 'same' as the last successful film venture.

It would appear in this light that the 'bridge' which Shakespeare creates between high and low culture is dictated to by the Hollywood marketplace. What Shakespeare 'means', at least in cinema, is governed by a stringent regime of industrial practices, as Chapter 3 indicated. Yet there are further issues at large in terms of film marketing. These issues are evidenced by the meticulous creation of a series of 'high school' Shakespeare films, each of which offer tie-ins with a further series of carefully constructed teen movies across a number of genres, and which therefore render Shakespeare both 'package-able' and predictable (see also French 2006: 16–22). Shakespeare 'means' in these films largely according to a studio-constructed system of Hollywood conservatism. Although this reading would appear to dismiss the agency of the spectator in making meaning from Shakespeare films, it is nonetheless important to recognise – as Morrissette's film makes clear – the ambivalence of Shakespeare's *cultural* identity in productions that deliberately market the Bard for both high and popular culture according to a series of homogenising market techniques.

Morrissette's film takes a long hard look at market strategies and capitalism by figuring the McBeth's rise to success (and moral descent) as an effort to go up in the material world. Their success is encapsulated in the form of Norm Duncan's usurped fast-food restaurant, in place of Duncan's kingdom in the play. Consider the importance of the restaurant's sign in this regard. At first, Norm's tatty eatery bears the family name in flashing lights as a marker of ownership and corporate identity. When the McBeths take it over they revamp the restaurant, replacing Norm's title with a huge 3-D red sign reading 'McBeths'– despite promising to Norm's son when purchasing the joint that they would 'keep the family name alive'. The exaggerated size of the 'McBeths' logo is suggestive of both its importance in the play and, more symbolically, the reinvention of Shakespeare's play – or possibly Shakespeare in general – as a commodity and commercial endeavour. Pointedly, much of the film's central action takes place around or actually on this logo. When Mac's guilty conscience gets the better of

Fig. 11: Keeping the family name alive: McBeth's brings fast food to the nation

him during the restaurant's public opening, the sign is prominently in view behind Mac as he reacts to Banko's (Kevin Corrigan) ghost. The show-down between Mac and McDuff transpires on the roof of the restaurant, upon which the hippies sit and from which McDuff leaps and seizes Mac, forcing him on to the bull horns on his car bonnet. By centralising the 'McBeth's' logo within the film's narrative and symbolic contexts, Morrissette indicates the importance of Shakespeare as a 'brand' or marketing logo in Hollywood and beyond.

In addition to its capitalist roots, the restaurant logo works in co-operation with the connective usage of 'Mac' to signify Shakespeare or, rather, to depict Shakespeare as a signifier detached from his original meaning. Like Duncan's 'lost' family name in the form of the replaced logo, Shakespeare's identity is replaced by cultural and commercial imperatives, while the original plays are suggested throughout the film as 'cannibalised' by popular culture. In addition, the number of citations, allusions and fashion statements throughout the film envelop Shakespeare's original in signifiers which persistently refer to historical periods and political upheavals (such as the Watergate scandal), as well as locations and intertexts other than Shakespeare. Film theorists such as Noël Carroll and John Biguenet have tended to view filmic allusion as a playful tendency that involves 'quotations, the memorialisation of past genres, the reworking of past genres, homages, and the recreation of "classic" scenes, shots, plot motifs, lines of dialogue, theme, gestures, and so forth from film history' (Carroll 1982: 152; see also Biguenet 1998). However, as Morrissette's film demonstrates, excessive allusion and allusion 'rather than experimentation' contains the threat of re-representing past-ness, deferring originality until 'the subject is *nothing but* the impossibility of its own signifying representation' (Žižek 1989: 208). Shakespeare's allusion and signified representation therefore runs the risk of 'signifying nothing' (5.5.28), displacing originality with a series of signs that 'mean' nothing, or everything but the original. To be sure, *Scotland, PA* presents a nostalgic glance at a moment of American history and at the upsurge of fast food, yet whereas Shakespeare is pitted against these features of popular culture as (another) appropriated element of consumer culture, he is never entirely engaged with as an 'original' text. This may be because Shakespeare's filmic representation is no longer possible as an unaffected work. Having been represented, performed and cited in myriad ways across popular culture, Shakespeare's representation requires the negotiation of many meanings, methods and market strategies that are specifically constructed to underline the Bard's cultural revival.

What this suggests is that Shakespeare 'for the people' is not entirely Hollywood's Shakespeare, yet by and large what we understand as 'popular' Shakespeare on film *is* determined by the Hollywood machine. An always unfixed signifier, 'Shakespeare' is not made more accessible by popular appropriations but instead serves to make transpositions between 'high' and 'low' culture accessible, or identifiable as the production of cultural practices that can be either hegemonic or transgressive. Culture is by nature hermeneutic; put differently, 'culture' is an apparatus of hermeneutics whereby exchanges between different groups of people can be interpreted and understood. By using Shakespeare as a map by which exchanges between high and low culture can be negotiated, *Scotland, PA* seeks to interpret and ultimately resist Shakespeare adaptation as a vehicle for imperialism, hegemony and social exclusion. Says Morrissette, the film offers a 'Shakespeare for the kid in the back row who is getting stoned, reading the Cliff Notes' (2002). This is presumably the kid who also identifies with low-paid employment at a burger bar, an obtuse father and, like school children around the world, an education that champions

Shakespeare as the greatest writer of all time without understanding why (see also Farouky 2006: 52). As Morrissette's film makes clear, the manufacturing of Shakespeare is just as important as reading the texts themselves if such an understanding is ever to be reached.

O-ing it all to Shakespeare

> I always feel, whenever I encounter a teen movie, that there is an elephant in the room that everyone is ignoring. The elephant is teen violence.
> – Tim Blake Nelson (quoted in LaSalle 2001)

Tim Blake Nelson's directorial debut, *O*, draws upon Shakespeare's *Othello* to address the growing problem of teen violence in North America. Between 1996 and 1999, 13 shooting incidents had occurred in high schools throughout the United States. Driven by these incidents, *O* was given the green light by Miramax and prepared for release in the spring of 1999, but was subsequently shelved for almost two years due to an unforeseen event that corresponded rather closely with Nelson's film. On 20 April 1999 high school students Eric Harris and Dylan Klebold armed themselves with a range of guns, blades and bombs, and entered Columbine High School in Jefferson County, Colorado. There they shot 34 students and teachers before committing suicide, killing 15 in total. The plan, apparently, had been to blow up the school and shoot fleeing survivors. Their propane bombs alone had the capacity to kill six hundred people (see Cullen 2004). As Nelson acknowledges, the *intent* behind each of the numerous US high school shootings – coupled with the actual casualty rate – registers both the seriousness of teen violence and a devastating copy-cat culture emerging across the world. With regards to the first of these concerns, websites, publications and documentaries spiralled in Columbine's wake, the main effort being to identify why two teenagers from apparently stable backgrounds had committed such a grievous crime. Fingers pointed immediately at features and figures of popular culture, such as Marilyn Manson, *The Matrix* and violent video games such as *Doom* and *Quake*, as well as social issues such as bullying, peer pressure, the teenage use of antidepressants and US gun laws. Following the Columbine massacre, 17 further high school shootings occurred in the US between 2000 and

2005, and the debate surrounding teen violence and its attendant issues remains unresolved. Blake Nelson's film aims to penetrate some of the central issues of this continuing copy-cat culture and, as the director put it to reluctant Miramax bosses, to 'illuminate the causes and consequences of high school violence' in the hope that the film could 'be constructive in dealing with the problem' (Mundhra 2001).

But why choose Shakespeare to address this problem? Blake Nelson never exactly makes his reasons clear. On the one hand, he admits his reluctance to take on Brad Kaaya's Shakespeare-inflected script in the first place: 'When I was told about this script, I really didn't want to be a part of it, because I felt that there was enough butchering of Shakespeare's plays by teening them down.' He goes on to say that 'I *hate* saying, "it's a high school adaptation of *Othello*". It feels so embarrassing' (quoted in Mundhra 2001). Yet a high school adaptation of *Othello* it is. Brad Kaaya's script drew upon his own experiences as the only black student at a US high school and invoked Shakespeare's play to articulate those experiences. In Kaaya's words, 'I love *Othello* and thought it would be a perfect fit and that I could do visual Cliff Notes' (quoted in Fetters 2001). Nelson's purposes in choosing 'visual Cliff Notes' of Shakespeare's play to re-contextualise a dominating social issue appear inconsistent with his chief objectives. That is, at first.

Set at a fictional high school, Palmetto Grove Academy, in America's Deep South, the film presents Othello, or O (short for Odin James (Mekhi Phifer)), as a talented teenage basketball player and the only black student at Palmetto Grove. As in Shakespeare's plot, O succumbs to Iago/Hugo's (Josh Hartnett) lies and murders his lover, Desdemona/Desi (Julia Stiles), daughter of the Dean. Despite Blake Nelson's hesitation to 'teen down' Shakespeare, the film's portraits of basketball culture, peer pressure, father/son and father/daughter relationships and high school violence rather predictably list the genre codes of the teen movie. In addition, the cast, fresh from appearances in *10 Things I Hate About You* (Julia Stiles and Andrew Keegan) and Michael Almereyda's *Hamlet* (Julia Stiles again), forges familiar territory for fans of teen Shakespeare films. However, it appears that these choices are necessary to register the varying contexts of and debates surrounding high school violence, as noted previously. Shakespeare, however, appears as an unnecessary ingredient that simply adds requisite drama and cultural value. Cited during the highly mediatised

O. J. Simpson murder trial of 1995 as a textual parallel, *Othello*'s presence in popular culture plays a vital part in the election of a (loose) Shakespeare adaptation to articulate teen violence. Already contextualised across a variety of performances, social issues and commodities, *Othello* offers the film apparently necessary contexts through which to investigate and 'deal with' a highly complex problem. Shakespeare's presence is rarely felt in the film – which was confirmed by the surprise of my fellow cinema-goers who had not realised the film's textual origins until I told them – but his contexts *are*. Though the film fails to achieve the impossible – that is, to really 'deal' with or solve the issue at hand – its presentation of a prevailing global problem is a compelling reminder of the need for action.

However, at times the disparity between the social ideologies underscoring Shakespeare's play, such as misogyny, 'otherness' and interracial relationships, and those of the twenty-first century make for an unconvincing plot, exposing the transposition from a high-culture early-modern text to contemporary popular culture. Odin and Desi's romance is convincing; Odin's motivation for murdering Desi is not. Odin's singularity at an all-white boarding school is – shockingly – convincing, as is Hugo's motivation for spinning a web of deceit. Yet the apparent point being made in the film about Odin's 'otherness' is never completely realised. At the end, a tearful O makes his final speech before Hugo and police officers without a word of apology. Instead, he tells Hugo 'I ain't no different than none y'all. My mama's no crackhead … You tell 'em where I'm from didn't make me do this', before turning the gun on himself. Suddenly desperate to prove himself as 'no different', Odin's last confession is intended to reference the perpetuation of racial stereotypes and racial hatred across North America, yet in the context of the film his confession has no currency. Unlike Kaaya, O has not experienced discrimination. The fact that Odin 'got played' by a 'white boy' has nothing to do with racial jealousy or hatred, but rather Hugo's jealousy at Odin's relationship with Hugo's father, who tactlessly announces before the whole school, 'I love him like my own son', and Hugo's general failure to achieve the same recognition as Odin. Add to that recipe the prevailing issue of class, as Blake Nelson eschews the usual public high school setting for a private boarding school for students who drive BMW convertibles (as does Hugo) or demonstrate exceptional talent to get free tuition (as does Odin). The film simply takes on too many issues to ever achieve impact in any one of these areas.

The issue of 'Shakespeare' – and indeed the meaning of the play – thus becomes problematised by the film's myriad contexts and intertextual glances. On the other hand, however, Shakespeare's presence in the film, while hard to define, suggests the Bard's 'popularity' or relevance to an area of critical cultural concern as an apposite meaning system. Shakespeare here serves as an O-shaped lens through which the complex encounters of contemporary high school issues and teen violence can be perceived, in the same moment as it forces the spectator to identify the urgency for perception followed by action. As Barbara Hodgdon points out, the film portrays the high school as 'a microcosm of a larger culture that idolises sports heroes' and that is 'shot through with violence' (2003: 99). Arguably, Shakespeare serves in the production as a textual microcosm that signifies the macrocosm of teen violence. In the film's signifying practices, the letter O is invested with numerous references: O for *Othello*, O for Odin, O for O. J. Simpson, O for object, O for Other and O as the shape of a basketball hoop. The director's meticulous (and occasionally overwrought) contexts for the signified O can be read in terms of a series of concentric circles, which moves from Shakespeare's play to the conceptual issues of objectivity and otherness at the heart of the film. Odin is objectified by Hugo, or rather persuaded to replace his own subjectivity with one that is duped, master-minded and ultimately rendered different. Shakespeare is not the film's primary interest, but is pushed to the film's outer layer of critical issues. It is arguable that the film's effort to contain the myriad issues it raises requires a cultural force such as Shakespeare to fence them in, in order to prevent the complexity and variety of related debates obscuring the overall meaning that Blake Nelson is trying to achieve.

Conclusions

Shakespeare's 'popularisation' is perceivable as pertaining to a complex system of cultural ideologies, marketing and the general search for meaning. When meaning cannot be created from scratch, it is repackaged under a different 'brand' name and sold. The methods by which meaning – or indeed Shakespeare – are reproduced, however, continually redefine and create new classifications of appropriation and popularisation that prompt the question of encountering Shakespeare on film 'by degrees', as well as finding suitable taxonomies to cope with the ever-developing forms of intertextuality and cultural activity surrounding the Bard. As I have demonstrated, *Scotland, PA* and *O* manipulate Shakespeare's plays for various purposes that are essentially rooted in a pop culture context. Yet these films are still somewhat ambivalent about the Bard; his cultural status is not definable, and he is certainly never confirmed as being (about) one thing or another.

On the other hand, however, there is an argument that, despite the films' substitution of the text for more contemporary dialogues and situations, the re-invention of Shakespeare's themes and narratives illuminates the text by offering timely and diverse contexts by which to re-explore it. *Scotland, PA*, for instance, re-fashions *Macbeth*'s preoccupations with time ('tomorrow and tomorrow and tomorrow' (5.5.19)) and food ('Chief nourisher in life's feast' (2.2.37–8)) via nostalgic glances at the 1970s and fast food. In addition, these dual concerns in the play are fused in Morrissette's film, as suggested by the sign in Duncan's restaurant that reads 'Time to Eat'. In many ways, Morrissette's latent engagement with the text's symbolic levels offers a corresponding context that at once answers to the 'cannibalising' of Shakespeare by popular culture and contemporary culture's obsession with the past, continually reprising fashions and endeavouring to 'look like the time' (1.5.62). In *O*, the film points up a social concern of great importance in the same moment as its discourses on race and otherness provide fresh perspectives on this issue in the play. In both cases, 'Shakespeare' is not just a marker of authority, but also a cultural 'text' with many ghosts and shades that helpfully gives meaning and understanding to current issues, and vice versa.

A consideration of whether or not a popular appropriation is 'Shakespeare' or not alerts us to the question surrounding foreign Shakespeare films which translate the language and offer different cultural perspectives on Shakespeare's themes: are *they* Shakespeare? Aki Käurismaki's Finnish version of *Hamlet*, *Hamlet liikemaailmassa* (*Hamlet Goes Business*, 1987), stages the play as an absurdist black comedy/*film noir*. The film's satiric take on capitalist society is evocative of *Scotland, PA*, yet its grim reflection of Finland's financial crisis during the 1980s and the ramifications of this crisis is not tongue-in-cheek. A social satire it is, but the film is also definitely 'Shakespeare'. Likewise, both Akira Kurosawa's Shakespeare adaptations, *Throne of Blood* and *Ran*, blend Japanese history with Shakespeare's literature. Both films are period pieces set during the

Sengoku Jidai, or sixteenth century civil wars in Japan, providing *Macbeth* and *King Lear* with culturally-specific historical contexts. In *Throne of Blood* and *Ran* Kurosawa calls upon the tradition of Japanese Noh theatre, which champions economy of expression and copious symbolism. The rewriting of *Macbeth* according to Japanese culture and aesthetics creates a powerful synthesis of Oriental and Western cultures, and, despite the imposition of cultural, historical and linguistic translations, there is no question that the film is *not* a derivative or Shakespeare off-shoot, but an 'authentic' appropriation in its own light. As Lanier observes of Kurosawa's films:

> All are routinely treated as Shakespeare films, even though they contain not a single word written by Shakespeare. The designation 'Shakespeare' serves, in other words, as a principle of categorisation and interpretation, a way of highlighting (or creating) qualities or themes regarded as essential to the plays. (2002: 9)

Perceivably, the designation of 'Shakespeare' in adaptation is similar to that in popularisation. As a meaning system, or a 'principle of categorisation and interpretation', Shakespeare offers popular culture a mechanism by which complex ideological positions and practices of consumption, reproduction and cultural interaction can be organised and understood.

Shakespeare's popular function, then, cannot be restricted to one or even two major forms. Instead, it is perceivable that the Bard serves the past-bound interests of contemporary popular culture, enabling engagement with various points of history and performances as far back as the sixteenth century. Shakespeare's continually re-contextualised themes additionally offer contemporary popular culture palimpsests or networks of meaning, which are especially fitting in a postmodern environment. In sum, Shakespeare's commodified presence across a spectrum of products and environments provides a unifying framework within which to communicate cross-cultural dynamics to a global audience.

NOTES

Introduction

1   All references to Shakespeare's plays throughout the following chapters are taken from *The Norton Shakespeare*, W. Cohen, S. Greenblatt, J. Howard and K. E. Maus (eds) (New York: W. W. Norton, 1997).

2   See ‹http://www.boxofficeguru.com/h.htm›; accessed 10 July 2006.

3   See ‹http://www.boxofficeguru.com/s.htm›; accessed 10 July 2006.

4   Though the alleged budget for this production ranges between US $8.5 million and US $13 million, Branagh confirms the budget of US $4 million on his DVD commentary accompanying the film. See ‹http://www.branaghcompendium.com/artic-indguard01.html›; accessed 10 July 2006; ‹http://www.imdb.com/title/tt0182295/business›; accessed 10 July 2006.

Chapter Two

1   'Fathering-forth' is Edward Said's term, as it appears in 'On Originality', *The World, the Text, and the Critic* (Cambridge, MA: Harvard University Press, 1983, 135).

2   'Extratextual referentiality' is Constantine Verevis' phrase, as it appears in his book *Film Remakes* (Edinburgh: Edinburgh University Press, 2005, 95).

3   The 'textuality' of early modern painting is indicated by Greenaway's observation: 'The average painting which was hung in the Royal Aca-

demy in the seventeenth century was probably accompanied by about 17 pages of text. Questions regarding text and the image are endemic to the English culture, and they are certainly my big concerns, as well. One of my great disappointments was to realise that 95 per cent of all images are illustrations of text. And even after the revolutions in painting in the nineteenth century, you still have to use words to describe paintings. Paintings are still given titles, which are basically textural, and which entirely colour the way in which the painting is viewed. So if you want to be a visual creator, it's a great frustration.' (Joshua Cody, Peter Greenaway interview, November 1994. On-line. Available at: ‹http://www.paristransatlantic.com/magazine/interviews/greenaway.html›; accessed 1 March 2006).

4   See *The Official Dogme 95 website*. On-line. Available at: ‹http://www.dogme95.dk/menu/menuset.htm›; accessed 10th July 2006.

Chapter 3

1   In addition to the elements discussed here, however, are make-up (Welles' controversial use of blackface to play the Moor) and format (Welles' use of black and white, which has been argued to be employed as a technique to 'reduce racial difference to the fundamentally cinematic grid of black-and-white photography' (Stone 2002: 189)).

2   As an additional intertextual reference, Hamlet's montage refers to an earlier production also starring Ethan Hawke: Andrew Niccol's *Gattaca* (1997). Here Hawke plays Vincent/Jerome – a genetically disadvantaged character in a futuristic society where good genes means a good future. To overcome this disadvantage, Vincent 'becomes' Jerome by adopting his appearance and appropriating his biological make-up where necessary: all to reach the stars. In Almereyda's film, shots 7 and 9 refer to *Gattaca*'s poster and DVD cover, which features the circular figures of a human cell and a planet conjoined. Summing up the film's interest in genetics and space travel, the image is recalled in Hamlet's montage to draw upon Hawke's character as a performer in a meticulously constructed self-narrative: a very different kind of montage.

3   This is demonstrated by the musical accompaniment used alongside 'silent' films, which gradually became synchronised with the narrative until 'talkies' came into being.

Chapter 4

1 *My Wife and Kids*, 'Crouching Mother, Hidden Father', Dir. Andy Cadiff,
   Wayans Bros. Entertainment, tx 30 October 2002.

2 For example, *Get Over It* (2001), *Orange County* (2002), *10 Things I Hate
   About You* (1999) and *O* (Tim Blake Nelson, 2001).

3 I am thinking here of *Hero* (2002), which was released in the US and
   UK two years after its initial release in China following a battle between
   Quentin Tarantino and studio bosses to grant the film a Western audience. Tarantino offered his name to introduce the film and (possibly) as
   a mark of authentication.

SOURCES AND RESOURCES

There are a vast number of Shakespeare sources on-line and elsewhere, certainly too many to account for here. However, I have identified a selection of resources that are particularly useful for researching Shakespeare on film.

On-line Resources

Gail M. Feldman, 'Adapting Shakespeare to Film'
http://www.insidefilm.com/shakespeare.html

Early Modern Culture – an electronic seminar
http://emc.eserver.org/default.html

Encyclopaedia Britannica's Guide to William Shakespeare
http://search.eb.com/shakespeare/esa/660002.html

The First Folio and Early Quartos of William Shakespeare
http://etext.lib.virginia.edu/shakespeare/folio/

Hamlet on the Ramparts
http://shea.mit.edu/ramparts/collections/upenn/index.htm

In Search of Shakespeare
http://www.pbs.org/shakespeare/educators/resources.html

The Kenneth Branagh Compendium
http://www.branaghcompendium.com/

Screenonline: Shakespeare on Screen
http://www.screenonline.org.uk/

The Shakespeare Resource Centre
http://www.bardweb.net/

Sh:in:E - Shakespeare in Europe
http://pages.unibas.ch/shine/

SHAKSPER: The Global Electronic Shakespeare Conference
http://www.shaksper.net/

Collections, Databases, and Archives

The Folger Shakespeare Library On-line
http://shakespeare.folger.edu/

The International Database of Shakespeare on Film, Television and Radio – British
Universities Film & Video Council (Director: Luke McKernan)
http://www.bufvc.ac.uk/databases/shakespeare/index.html

The Kenneth Branagh Archive – The Queen's University of Belfast (Director:
Professor Mark Thornton Burnett)

The Shakespeare Institute – The University of Birmingham
http://www.shakespeare.bham.ac.uk/researchcollections.htm

The Shakespeare Birthplace Trust Library
http://www.shakespeare.org.uk/library.htm

Touchstone
http://www.touchstone.bham.ac.uk/

Current Journals

Borrowers and Lenders: The Journal of Shakespeare and Appropriation
www.borrowers.uga.edu/

Early Modern Literary Studies
http://www.shu.ac.uk/emls/emlshome.html

Literature/Film Quarterly – devotes one issue per year to the topic of Shakespeare on Film, usually in April
http://www.salisbury.edu/lfq/

Shakespeare
http://www.tandf.co.uk/journals/titles/17450918.asp

Shakespeare Quarterly
http://www.jstor.org/journals/00373222.html

Shakespeare Yearbook
http://www.sbg.ac.at/ang/projects/yearbook.htm

Shakespeare Magazine
http://www.shakespearemag.com/

Shakespeare Survey
http://www.cambridge.org/features/literature/shakespearesurvey/

Shakespeare in Southern Africa
http://www.ru.ac.za/institutes/isea/shake/journal.html

The Upstart Crow: A Shakespeare Journal
http://www.clemson.edu/caah/cedp/crow/

Conferences/Associations

Australian and New Zealand Shakespeare Association
(http://www.arts.unsw.edu.au/conferences/anzsa/) Meets every two years at various locations throughout Australia and New Zealand

The British Shakespeare Association
(http://www.britishshakespeare.ws/) Holds a conference every two years in Great Britain

The International Shakespeare Association
(http://www.shakespeare.org.uk/) Holds a World Shakespeare Congress every five years in various locations around the world

Shakespeare Association of America
(http://www.shakespeareassociation.org/) Holds a yearly conference in the USA

The Shakespeare Society of Southern Africa
(http://www.ru.ac.za/institutes/isea/shake/conference.html) Holds a congress every three years at Rhodes University, Grahamstown, South Africa

FILMOGRAPHY

Blade Runner (Ridley Scott, 1982, US)
Citizen Kane (Orson Welles, 1941, US)
Crouching Tiger, Hidden Dragon (Ang Lee, 2000, Taiwan/Hong Kong/UK/China)
Deliver Us From Eva (Gary Hardwick, 2003, US)
Fatal Attraction (Adrian Lyne, 1987, US)
Full Metal Jacket (Stanley Kubrick, 1987, US)
Gattaca (Andrew Niccol, 1997, US)
Get Over It (Tommy O'Haver, 2001, US)
Hamlet: A Drama of Vengeance (Svend Gade and Heinz Schall, 1920, Germany)
Hamlet (Laurence Olivier, 1948, UK)
Hamlet (Grigori Kozintsev, 1964, Soviet Union/US)
Hamlet (Franco Zeffirelli, 1990, US)
Hamlet (Kenneth Branagh, 1996, UK/US)
Hamlet (Michael Almereyda, 2000, US)
Hamlet liikemaailmassa (*Hamlet Goes Business*) (Aki Käurismaki, 1987, Finland)
Henry V (Laurence Olivier, 1944, UK)
Henry V (Kenneth Branagh, 1989, UK)
Jaws (Steven Spielberg, 1975, US)
King of Texas (Uli Edel, 2002, US)
King Is Alive, The (Kristian Levring, 2000, Denmark)
King John (Herbert Beerbohm Tree, 1899, UK)
Kumonosu jô (*Throne of Blood*) (Akira Kurosawa, 1957, Japan)
Lethal Weapon (Richard Donner, 1987, US)
Lord of the Rings: The Fellowship of the Ring (Peter Jackson, 2001, US/NZ)
Love's Labour's Lost (Kenneth Branagh, 2000, France/UK/Canada)
Macbeth: The Comedy (Allison L. LiCalsi, 2001, US)
Mad Max (George Miller, 1979, Australia)

Mad Max Beyond Thunderdome (George Miller and George Ogilvie, 1985, US/Australia)

Maqbool (Vishal Bharadwaj, 2003, India)

Matrix, The (The Wachowski Bros., 1999, US)

Merchant of Venice, The (Michael Radford, 2004, UK)

Midsummer Night's Dream, A (Michael Hoffman, 1999, US)

Midsummer Night's Rave, A (Gil Cates, 2002, US)

Moulin Rouge! (Baz Luhrmann, 2001, Australia/US)

My Kingdom (Don Boyd, 2001, Italy/UK)

O (Tim Blake Nelson, 2001, US)

Omen III: The Final Conflict, The (Graham Baker, 1981, US)

Orange County (Jake Kasdan, 2002, US)

Othello (Oliver Parker, 1995, US)

Pillow Book, The (Peter Greenaway, 1996, UK)

Platoon (Oliver Stone, 1986, US)

Prospero's Books (Peter Greenaway, 1991, France/Netherlands/UK/Japan)

Ran (Akira Kurosawa, 1985, Japan/France)

Rave Macbeth (Klaus Knoesel, 2001, Germany)

Rêve de Shakespeare, Le (Georges Méliès, 1907, France)

Richard III (Richard Loncraine, 1995, UK/US)

Romeo and Juliet (Franco Zeffirelli, 1968, Italy/US)

Scarface (Brian de Palma, 1983, US)

Scotland, PA. (Billy Morrissette, 2001, US)

Seven Year Itch, The (Billy Wilder, 1955, US)

Shakespeare in Love (John Madden, 1998, US)

Spellbound (Alfred Hitchcock, 1945, US)

Star Wars (George Lucas, 1977, US)

Star Wars: Macbeth (Bien Concepcion and Donald Fitz-Roy, 1998, US)

Street King, The (James Gavin Bedford, 2002, US)

Strictly Ballroom (Baz Luhrmann, 1992, Australia)

Teenage Mutant Ninja Turtles, The (Steve Barron, 1990, US/Hong Kong)

10 Things I Hate About You (Gil Junger, 1999, US)

Titus (Julie Taymor, 1999, Italy/US)

Tragedy of Othello: The Moor of Venice, The (Orson Welles, 1952, US/Italy/France)

Tromeo and Juliet (Lloyd Kaufmann, 1996, US)

William Shakespeare's Romeo + Juliet (Baz Luhrmann, 1996, US)

Wuthering Heights (William Wyler, 1939, US)

Ying xiong (Hero) (Yimou Zhang, 2002, China)

BIBLIOGRAPHY

This initial list includes all works cited in the text

Abbot, S. H. (1997) 'Interview with Peter Greenaway', *Chris Renson*. On-line. Available at: ‹http://users.skynet.be/chrisrenson-makemovies/Greenaw3. htm›; accessed 22 May 2007.

Adamek, P. (1996) 'Interview with Baz Luhrmann', *The Dream Page*. On-line. Available at: ‹http://www.dicapriodreams.com/Leo/baz.html›; accessed 1 October 2006.

Andrew, D. (1984) *Concepts in Film Theory*. Oxford: Oxford University Press.

Andrew, G. (2001) 'Baz Luhrmann Interview', *The Guardian Online*. On-line. Available at: ‹http://film.guardian.co.uk/interview/interviewpages/0,,548458,00. html›; accessed 1 January 2007.

Arnheim, R. (1957) *Film as Art*. Berkeley: University of California Press.

Arnold, G. (1996) 'Branagh Breathes New Life into Classics', *Insight on the News*, 36–7.

Astruc, A. (1948) 'Birth of a New Avant-Garde: La Caméra-Stylo', *L'Ecran Français*, 144.

Aumont, J., A. Bergala, M. Marie and M. Vernet (1994) *Aesthetics of Film*, trans. and rev. by R. Neupert. Austin: University of Texas Press.

Babcock, R. W. (1964) *The Genesis of Shakespeare Idolatry, 1766–1799: A Study in English Criticism of the Late Eighteenth Century*. New York: Russell & Russell.

Ball, R. H. (1968) *Shakespeare on Silent Film: A Strange Eventful History*. London: George Allen and Unwin.

Barthes, R. (1995 [1968]) 'The Death of the Author', in S. Burke (ed.) *Authorship: From Plato to the Postmodern: A Reader*. Edinburgh: Edinburgh University Press, 125–30.

Bazin, A. (1967) *What is Cinema?* Vol. 1, trans. Hugh Gray. Berkeley: University of

California Press.

Bazin, A. (1973) *What is Cinema?* Trans. Hugh Gray. Vol. 2. Berkeley: University of California Press.

Benjamin, W. (1969) *Illuminations*. New York: Schocken Books.

Biguenet, J. (1998) 'Double Takes: The Role of Allusion in Cinema', in A. Horton and S. McDougal (eds) *Play It Again, Sam: Retakes on Remakes*. Berkeley: University of California Press, 131–43.

Billington, M. (1996 'Was Shakespeare English?', in H. Kerr, R. Eaden and M. Mitton (eds) *Shakespeare: World Views*. London: Associated University Presses, 15–28.

Bloom, H. (1973) *The Anxiety of Influence: A Theory of Poetry*. New York: Oxford University Press.

_____ (1975) *A Map of Misreading*. New York: Oxford University Press.

Bordwell, D. (1997) *On the History of Film Style*. Cambridge and London: University of Wisconsin Press.

Bordwell, D. and K. Thompson (1997) *Film Art: An Introduction* (fifth edition). London and New York: McGraw Hill.

Bristol. M. (1996) *Big-Time Shakespeare*. New York and London: Routledge.

Buchanan, J. (2005) *Shakespeare on Film*. London: Longman Pearson.

Burnett, M. T. (2005) 'Writing Shakespeare in the Global Economy', *Shakespeare Survey*, 58, 185–98.

Burnett, M. T. and R. Wray (2000) 'From the Horse's Mouth: Branagh on the Bard', in M. T. Burnett and R. Wray (eds) *Shakespeare, Film, Fin de Siècle*. Basingstoke: Macmillan, 165–78.

Burt, R. (2002) 'Afterword: Te(e)n Things I Hate about Girlene Shakesploitation Flicks in the Late 1990s, or Not-So-Fast Times at Shakespeare High', in C. Lehmann and L. S. Starks (eds) *Spectacular Shakespeare: Critical Theory and Popular Cinema*. Madison: Fairleigh Dickinson University Press, 205–32.

Carroll, N. (1982) 'The Future of Allusion: Hollywood in the Seventies (and Beyond)', *October*, 20, 151–81.

_____ (1988) *Interpreting the Moving Image*. Cambridge: Cambridge University Press.

Cartmell, D. (1999) 'The Shakespeare on Screen Industry', in D. Cartmell and I. Whelehan (eds) *Adaptations: From Text to Screen, Screen to Text*. London and New York: Routledge, 29–37.

Casetti, F. (1999) *Theories of Cinema 1945–1995*. Trans. F. Chiostri and E. Gard Bartolini-Salimbeni with T. Kelso. Austin: University of Texas Press.

Castellitto, G. P. (1998) 'Imagism and Martin Scorsese: Images Suspended and Extended', *Literature/Film Quarterly*, 26, 1, 23–9.

Chion, M. (1999) *The Voice in Cinema*. Trans. Claudia Gorbman. New York:

Columbia University Press.

Chura, P. (2000) '*Hamlet* and the Failure of Soviet Authority in Lithuania', *Lituanus*. On-line. Available at: ‹http://www.lituanus.org/2000/00_4_02.htm›; accessed 1 March 2006.

Cody, J. (1994) 'Interview with Peter Greenaway'. On-line. Available at: ‹http://www.paristransatlantic.com/magazine/interviews/greenaway.html›; accessed 1 March 2006.

Cohen, W., S. Greenblatt, J. Howard and K. E. Maus (eds) (1997) *The Norton Shakespeare*. New York: W. W. Norton.

Crowl, S. (1994) '*Hamlet* "Most Royal": An Interview with Kenneth Branagh', *Shakespeare Bulletin*, 12, 4, 5–8.

Cullen, D. (2004) 'The Depressive and the Psychopath: At last we know why the Columbine killers did it', *Slate*, 20 April. On-line. Available at ‹http://www.slate.com/id/2099203/›; accessed 21 April 2006.

Debord, G. (1995 [1967]) *The Society of the Spectacle*, trans. D. Nicholson-Smith. London: Zone Books.

Deelman, C. (1964) *The Great Shakespeare Jubilee*. New York: Viking Press.

Derrida, J. (1978) *Writing and Difference*, trans. Alan Bass. London and New York: Routledge.

____ (1979) 'Living On', in J. Julbart (ed.) *Deconstruction and Criticism: A Continuum Book*. New York: Seabury Press, 75–176.

Doane, M. A. (1999) 'The Voice In The Cinema', in L. Braudy and M. Cohen (eds) *Film Theory and Criticism: Introductory Readings*. Fifth Edition. New York and Oxford: Oxford University Press, 363–75.

Donaldson, P. (1990) *Shakespearean Films/Shakespearean Directors*. Boston: Unwin Hyman.

Dorval, P. (2000) 'Shakespeare on Screen: Threshold Aesthetics in Oliver Parker's *Othello*', *Early Modern Literary Studies*, 6, 1, 1–15. On-line. Available at: ‹http://purl.oclc.org/emls/06-1/dorvothe.htm›; accessed 1 May 2006.

Dyer, R. (1987) *Heavenly Bodies: Film Stars and Society*. London: British Film Institute.

Ebert, R. (2002) '*Scotland PA* Review'. On-line. Available at: ‹http://rogerebert.suntimes.com/apps/pbcs.dll/article?AID=/20020215/REVIEWS/202150307/1023›; accessed 1 May 2006.

Eco, U. (1994) *Reflections on 'The Name of the Rose'*, trans. William Weaver. London: Minerva.

Eisenstein, S. (1949) *Film Form: Essays in Film Theory*, ed. and trans. Jay Leyda. New York: Harcourt Brace.

Eliot, T. S. (1996 [1917]) 'The Love Song of J. Alfred Prufrock', in A. W. Allison, M. J. Salter, J. Stallworthy and M. W. Ferguson (eds) *The Norton Anthology of Poetry*.

New York: W. W. Norton, 1230.

Epstein, N. (1993) *The Friendly Shakespeare*. New York: Viking.

Esslin, M. (1971) *The Man and His Work*. New York: Doubleday.

Farouky, J. (2006) 'Shakespeare Inc.', *Time Europe*, 67, 13, 52–8.

Fetters, S. M. (2001) 'Seattle International Film Festival Coverage'. On-line. Available at: ‹http://www.moviefreak.com/features/siff2001/seattlefilm04.htm›; accessed 10 May 2006.

Foucault, M. (1977 [1970]) 'What is an Author?', trans. D. F. Bouchard and S. Simon, in D. F. Bouchard (ed.) Language, Counter-Memory, Practice. New York: Cornell University Press, 124–7.

French, E. (2006) *Selling Shakespeare to Hollywood: The Marketing of Filmed Shakespeare Adaptations from 1989 the New Millennium*. Hatfield, Herts: University of Hertfordshire Press.

Freud, S. (1959 [1909]) 'Family Romances', in *The Standard Edition of the Complete Psychological Works of Sigmund Freud*, Vol. 9, trans. and ed. James Strachey. London: Hogarth Press, 237–41.

_____ (1995 [1919]) 'The Uncanny', in *The Standard Edition of the Complete Psychological Works of Sigmund Freud*, Vol. 17, trans. and Ed. James Strachey. London: Hogarth Press, 217–52.

Genette, G. (1997) *Palimpsests: Literature in the Second Degree*. Lincoln, NE: University of Nebraska Press.

Geraghty, C. (2000) 'Re-examining stardom: Questions of text, bodies and performance', in C. Gledhill and L. Williams (eds) *Reinventing Film Studies*. London: Arnold, 183–201.

Gollancz, I. (1916) (ed.) *A Book of Homage to Shakespeare*. Oxford: Oxford University Press.

Greenaway, P. (1991) *Prospero's Books: A Film of Shakespeare's 'The Tempest'*. New York: Four Walls Eight Windows.

Greene, R. (1592) *Groatsworth of Witte*. London: William Wright. On-line. Available at ‹http://darkwing.uoregon.edu/~rbear/greene1.html›; accessed 1 May 2006.

Habicht, W. (2001) 'Shakespeare Celebrations in Times of War', *Shakespeare Quarterly*, 52, 4, 441–55.

Hamilton, L. (2002) 'Baz versus the Bardolaters, or Why *William Shakespeare's Romeo + Juliet* Deserves Another Look', in J. M. Welsh, R. Vela and J. C. Tibbetts (eds) *Shakespeare Into Film*. New York: Facts on File, 159–66.

Hawkes, T. (1992) *Meaning By Shakespeare*. London and New York: Routledge.

Hawthorne, C. (1997) 'The Salon Interview: Peter Greenaway'. On-line. Available at: ‹http://www.salon.com/june97/greenaway2970606.html›; accessed 1 May 2006.

Hoberman, J. (2002) 'Blood Simple'. On-line. Available at: ‹http://www.villa-gevoice.com/film/0206,hoberman,32058,20.html›; accessed 1 May 2006.

Hodgdon, B. (1998) *The Shakespeare Trade: Performances and Appropriations*. Philadelphia: University of Pennsylvania Press.

____ (2003) 'Race-ing *Othello*, re-engendering white-out, II', in R. Burt and L. E. Boose (eds) *Shakespeare, the Movie, II: Popularising the Plays on Film, TV, Video and DVD*. London and New York: Routledge, 89–104.

Hotchkiss, L. M. (2002) 'The Incorporation of Word as Image in Peter Greenaway's Prospero's Books', in L. S. Starks and C. Lehmann (eds) *The Reel Shakespeare: Alternative Cinema and Theory*. Madison, NJ: Fairleigh Dickinson University Press/London: Associated University Presses, 95–117.

Iser, W. (1978) *The Act of Reading: A Theory of Aesthetic Response*. Baltimore: Johns Hopkins University Press.

Jameson, F. (1988 [1982]) 'Postmodernism and Consumer Society', in E. Ann Kaplan (ed.) *Postmodernism and Its Discontents*. New York: Verso, 13–58.

Jenkins, H. (1992) *Textual Poachers: Television Fans and Participatory Culture*. London: Routledge.

Jorgens, J. (1991 [1976]) *Shakespeare on Film*. Lanham: University Press of America.

Kahn, C. (2001) 'Remembering Shakespeare Imperially: The 1916 Tercentenary', *Shakespeare Quarterly*, 52, 4, 456–78.

Klevan, A. (2005) *Film Performance: From Achievement to Appreciation*. London: Wallflower Press.

Kott, J. (1967) *Shakespeare Our Contemporary*, trans. B. Taborski. London: Methuen.

Kozintsev, G. (1966) *Shakespeare: Time and Conscience*. New York: Hill & Wang.

Kracauer, S. (1995 [1947]) *Theory of Film: The Redemption of Physical Reality*. Princeton: Princeton University Press.

Landow, G. (1991) *Hypertext: The Convergence of Contemporary Critical Theory and Technology*. Baltimore: Johns Hopkins University Press.

Lanier, D. (2002) *Shakespeare in Modern Popular Culture*. Oxford: Oxford University Press.

____ (2006) 'Will of the People: Recent Shakespeare Film Parody and the Politics of Popularisation', in D. E. Henderson (ed.) *A Concise Companion to Shakespeare on Screen*. Oxford: Blackwell, 176–96.

LaSalle, M. (2001) 'Director Tim Blake Nelson's controversial O mirrors high-school violence', *San Francisco Chronicle*. On-line. Available at: ‹http://www.sfgate.com/cgi-bin/article.cgi?f=/c/a/2001/09/02/PK133125.DTL&type=movies›; accessed 9 May 2006.

Lehmann, C. (2005) 'The Passion of the "W": Provincializing Shakespeare,

Globalizing Manifest Density from King Lear to Kingdom Come', *The Upstart Crow*, 25, 16–32.

Lehmann, C. and L. S. Starks (2000) 'Making Mother Matter: Repression, Revision, and the Stakes of "Reading Psychoanalysis Into" Kenneth Branagh's *Hamlet*', *Early Modern Literary Studies*, 6, 1, 1–24. On-line. Available at: ⟨http://purl.oclc.org/emls/06-1/lehmhaml.htm⟩; accessed 1 June 2006.

Lumet, S. (1995) *Making Movies*. London: Bloomsbury.

McAlpine, D. (2006) 'Cinematographer's Gallery: Scene Studies', *William Shakespeare's Romeo + Juliet* (Baz Luhrmann, 1996), Special Edition DVD, 20th Century Fox.

Maltby, R. (2003) *Hollywood Cinema*, second edition. London: Blackwell.

Manovich, L. (2002) *The Language of New Media*. Cambridge: MIT Press.

Metz, C. (1974) *Film Language*, trans. Michael Taylor. Oxford and New York: Oxford University Press.

Monaco, J. (1981) *How to Read a Film: The Art, Technology, Language, History and Theory of Film and Media*. Oxford: Oxford University Press.

Morrissette, B. (2002) *Scotland, PA*: Press Kit. On-line. Available at ⟨http://lot47.com/scotlandpa/press_shakespeare.html⟩; accessed 1 March 2006.

Mundhra, S. (2001) 'All About O', *IGN*. On-line. Available at: ⟨http://uk.filmforce.ign.com/articles/305/305422p1.html⟩; accessed 10 May 2006.

Murphy, A. (2000) 'The Book on the Screen: Shakespeare Films and Textual Culture', in M. T. Burnett and R. Wray (eds) *Shakespeare, Film, Fin de Siècle*. Basingstoke: Macmillan, 10–25.

Murray, B. (2005) *Shakespeare Adaptations from the Restoration: Five Plays*. Madison and Teaneck: Fairleigh Dickinson University Press.

Naremore, J. (ed.) (2000) *Film Adaptation*. London: Athlone.

Olivier, L. (1982) *Confessions of an Actor*. London: Weidenfeld and Nicolson.

Orpen, V. (2003) *Film Editing: The Art of the Expressive*. London: Wallflower Press.

Pearce, C. and B. Luhrmann (1996) *William Shakespeare's Romeo + Juliet: The Contemporary Film, The Classic Play*. New York: Laurel Leaf.

Perkins, V. (1993) *Film as Film*. New York: Da Capo Press.

Rothwell, K. S. (2002) '*Hamlet* in Silence: Reinventing the Prince on Celluloid', in L. S. Starks and C. Lehmann (eds) *The Reel Shakespeare: Alternative Cinema and Theory*. Madison and Teaneck: Fairleigh Dickinson University Press/ London: Associated University Presses, 25–40.

____ (2004) *A History of Shakespeare on Screen: A Century of Film and Television*, second edition. Cambridge: Cambridge University Press.

Rundle, P. (1999) 'Interview with Kristian Levring'. On-line. Available at: ⟨http://www.tvropa.com/tvropa1.2/film/dogma95/menu/menuset.htm⟩; accessed 1 March 2006.

Said, E. W. (1983) 'On Originality', in *The World, the Text, and the Critic*. Cambridge, MA: Harvard University Press, 126–39.

Shaw, G. B. (1931 [1901]) *Three Plays for Puritans*. London: Constable, i–xx.

Smith, M. (1995) *Engaging Characters: Fiction, Emotion and the Cinema*. Oxford: Clarendon Press.

Stam, R. (2000) 'Beyond Fidelity: The Dialogics of Adaptation', in J. Naremore (ed.) *Film Adaptation*. London: Athlone, 54–78.

____ (2005) 'Introduction: The Theory and Practice of Adaptation', in R. Stam and A. Raengo (eds) *Literature and Film: A Guide to the Theory and Practice of Film Adaptation*. Oxford: Blackwell, 1–52.

Stone, J. W. (2002) 'Black and White as Technique in Orson Welles' *Othello*', in J. M. Welsh, R. Vela and J. C. Tibbetts (eds) *Shakespeare Into Film*. New York: Facts on File, 189–92.

Storey, J. (2003) *Inventing Popular Culture: From Folklore to Globalisation*. London: Blackwell.

Swain, H (1997) 'Why Will was no great', *Times Higher Education Supplement*, 24 January 1997, 18–19.

Taylor, G. (1990) *Reinventing Shakespeare: A Cultural History from the Restoration to the Present*. London: Hogarth Press.

Taymor, J. (2000) *Titus: The Illustrated Screenplay*. New York: Newmarket Press.

Tibbetts, J. C. (2002) 'Backstage with the Bard, or, Building a Better Mousetrap', in J. M. Welsh, R. Vela and J. C. Tibbetts (eds) *Shakespeare into Film*. New York: Facts on Film, 207–27.

Toulet, E. (1995) *Cinema is 100 Years Old*. London: Thames and Hudson.

Tweedie, J. (2000) 'Caliban's Books: The Hybrid Text in Peter Greenaway's *Prospero's Books*', *Cinema Journal*, 40, 1, 104–26.

Verevis, C. (2005) *Film Remakes*. Edinburgh: Edinburgh University Press.

Vincendeau, G. (ed.) (2001) 'Introduction', in *Film/Literature/Heritage: A Sight and Sound Reader*. London: British Film Institute, xi–xxvi.

Von Trier, L. and T. Vinterberg (2000) 'Dogme 95 manifesto', in *p.o.v: A Danish Journal of Film Studies*, 10, 6–7.

Weideli, W. (1963) *The Art of Bertolt Brecht*. London: Merlin.

Wells, S. (1995) *Shakespeare: A Life in Drama*. London and New York: W. W. Norton & Co.

Žižek, S. (1989) *The Sublime Object of Ideology*. London and New York: Verso.

Suggested further reading

Aebischer, P. (ed.) (2003) *Remaking Shakespeare: Performance Across Media, Genres and Cultures*. New York and Basingstoke: Palgrave.

Almereyda, M. (2000) *William Shakespeare's 'Hamlet': A Screenplay Adaptation by Michael Almereyda*. London: Faber and Faber.

Baudry, J. L. (1986 [1976]) 'The Apparatus: Metapsychological Approaches to the Impression of Reality in the Cinema', in Philip Rosen (ed.) *Narrative, Apparatus, Ideology: A Film Theory Reader*. New York: Columbia University Press, 299–318.

Bloom, H. (1994) 'Freud: A Shakespearean Reading', in *The Western Canon: The Books and School of the Ages*. New York: Harcourt Brace & Company, 371–94.

Bluestone, G. (2001) *Novels into Film*. Baltimore: John Hopkins University Press.

Branagh, K. (1996) *Hamlet, By William Shakespeare: Screenplay, Introduction, and Film Diary*. New York: W. W. Norton and Company.

Bristol, M. (1990) *Shakespeare's America, America's Shakespeare*. London: Routledge.

Burnett, M. T. (2002) '"We are the makers of manners": The Branagh Phenomenon', in Richard Burt (ed.) *Shakespeare After Mass Media*. London: Palgrave, 83–103.

_____ (2003) '"To hear and see the matter": Communicating Technology in Michael Almereyda's *Hamlet*', *Cinema Journal*, 42, 3, 48–69.

Burt, R. (1999) *Unspeakable Shakespeares*. New York and Basingstoke: Palgrave.

_____ (2002) *Shakespeare After Mass Media*. New York and Basingstoke: Palgrave.

_____ (2006) *Shakespeares after Shakespeare: An Encyclopedia of the Bard in Mass Media and Popular Culture*. Westport: Greenwood Publishing Group.

Cardwell, S. (2002) *Adaptation Revisited: Television and the Classic Novel*. Manchester: Manchester University Press.

Cartmell D., I. Q. Hunter and I. Whelehan (eds) (2001) *Retrovisions: Reinventing the Past in Film and Fiction*. London: Pluto Press.

Crofts, S. (1998) 'Authorship and Hollywood', in John Hill and Pamela Church Gibson (eds) *The Oxford Guide to Film Studies*. New York and Oxford: Oxford University Press, 310–27.

Crowl, S. (2003) *Shakespeare at the Cineplex: The Branagh Era*. Athens: Ohio University Press.

Dobson, M. (1992) *The Making of the National Poet: Shakespeare, Adaptation, and Authorship, 1660–1769*. Oxford: Clarendon.

Elliott, K. (2003) *Rethinking the Novel/Film Debate*. Cambridge: Cambridge University Press.

Gibbs, J. (2002) *Mise-en-Scène: Film Style and Interpretation*. London and New York: Wallflower Press.

Gibbs, J. and D. Pye. (2005) 'Introduction', in J. Gibbs and D. Pye (eds) *Style and Meaning: Studies in the Detailed Analysis of Film*. Manchester: Manchester

University Press.

Giddings, R., K. Selby and C. Wensley (1990) *Screening the Novel: Theory and Practice of Literary Dramatisation*. Basingstoke: Palgrave Macmillan.

Hatchuel, S. (2000) *A Companion to the Shakespearean Films of Kenneth Branagh*. Winnipeg: Blizzard.

Henderson, D. E. (ed.) (2006) *A Concise Companion to Shakespeare on Screen*. London: Blackwell.

____ (2006) *Collaborations with the Past: Reshaping Shakespeare across Time and Media*. New York: Cornell University Press.

Howlett, K. (2000) *Framing Shakespeare on Film*. Athens: Ohio University Press.

Kewes, P. (1998) *Authorship and Appropriation: Writing for the Stage in England, 1660–1710*. Oxford: Clarendon Press.

Kingsley-Smith, J. E. (2002) 'Shakespearean Authorship in Popular British Cinema', *Literature/Film Quarterly*, 30, 3, 158–65.

Lanier, D. (1996) 'Drowning the Book: Prospero's Books and the Textual Shakespeare', in J. C. Bulman (ed.) *Shakespeare, Theory and Performance*, London and New York: Routledge, 187–209.

Lehmann, C. (2002) 'The Machine in the Ghost: *Hamlet*'s Cinematographic Kingdom', in *Shakespeare Remains: Theater to Film, Early Modern to Postmodern*. New York: Cornell University Press, 89–129.

____ (2006) 'What is an Adaptation? Or, How do you like your Shakespeare?', in R. Burt (ed.) *Shakespeares After Shakespeare: An Encyclopedia of the Bard in Mass Media and Popular Culture*. Westport, CT: Greenwood Press.

Levine, L. W. (1988) *Highbrow/Lowbrow: The Emergence of Cultural Hierarchy in America*. Cambridge, MA: Harvard University Press.

McDonald, P. (1998) 'Film Acting', in J. Hill and P. C. Gibson (eds) *The Oxford Guide to Film Studies*. Oxford: Oxford University Press, 30–5.

McFarlane, B. (1996) *Novel to Film: An Introduction to the Theory of Adaptation* Gloucestershire: Clarendon Press.

Maguire, Nancy Klein (1991) 'Nahum Tate's *King Lear*: "The King's Blest Restoration"', in Jean I. Marsden (ed.) *The Appropriation of Shakespeare: Post-Renaissance Reconstructions of the Works and the Myth*. Hertfordshire: Harvester Wheatsheaf, 29–39.

Marowitz, C. (1987) 'Shakespeare Recycled', *Shakespeare Quarterly*, 38, 4, 467–78.

Marx, S. (2001) 'Greenaway's Books', *Early Modern Literary Studies*, 7, 2, 1–22. On-line. Available at: <http://purl.oclc.org/emls/07-2/marxgree.htm>; accessed 1 February 2006.

Massai, S. (2005) *World-Wide Shakespeares: Local Appropriations in Film and Performance*. London: Routledge.

Montrose, L. (1996) *The Purpose of Playing: Shakespeare and the Cultural Politics of the Elizabeth Theatre*. Chicago: University of Chicago Press.

Novy, M. (2000) *Transforming Shakespeare: Contemporary Women's Re-Visions in Literature and Performance*. New York and Basingstoke: Palgrave.

Reynolds, B. (2003) *Performing Transversally: Reimagining Shakespeare and the Critical Future*. Basingstoke: Palgrave.

Rowe, K. (2003) '"Remember me": technologies of memory in Michael Almereyda's *Hamlet*', in R. Burt and L. E. Boose (eds) *Shakespeare, the Movie, II: Popularising the Plays in Film, TV, Video and DVD*. London and New York: Routledge, 37–55.

Ryan, K. (2001) 'Shakespeare and the Future', in D. Cartmell and M. Scott (eds) *Talking Shakespeare: Shakespeare into the Millennium*. Basingstoke: Palgrave, 187–200.

Starks, L. S. (2002) '"Remember me": Psychoanalysis, Cinema, and the Crisis of Modernity', *Shakespeare Quarterly*, 53, 2, 181–200.

Storey, J. (2006) *Cultural Theory and Popular Culture: A Reader*. Harlow: Prentice Hall.

Thompson, A. (1997) 'Asta Nielsen and the Mystery of *Hamlet*', in L. E. Boose and R. Burt (eds) *Shakespeare, the Movie: Popularising the Plays on Film, TV and Video*. London and New York: Routledge, 215–24.

Tibbetts, J. C. (2002) '"Every Project Has Its Season": Mel Gibson and Franco Zeffirelli on the Challenges of *Hamlet*', in J. M. Welsh, R. Vela and J. C. Tibbetts (eds) *Shakespeare Into Film*. New York: Facts on File, 125–8.

Wagner, G. (1989) *The Novel and the Cinema*. Madison: Farleigh Dickinson Press.

Weller, P. (1997) 'Freud's Footprints in Films of *Hamlet*', *Literature-Film Quarterly*, 25, 2, 119–25.

Wilson, R. F. (2000) *Shakespeare in Hollywood 1929–1956*. Teaneck: Farleigh Dickinson Press.

Worthen, W. B. (1997) *Shakespeare and the Authority of Performance*. Cambridge: Cambridge University Press.

INDEX